Welcome to the course

Welcome to Modern World History. Studying this subject will help you to understa_____ in: the events of the last century can help to explain the problems and opportunities that exist in the world today.

How to use this book

There are four units in the course and each is worth 25% of the whole GCSE. This book covers Unit 3C The transformation of British society c.1951–79. There are four key topics in this unit and you will study *all four*.

- **Key Topic 1:** British society and economy in the 1950s
- **Key Topic 2:** Education, work and labour relations 1960–79
- **Key Topic 3:** Media, communications and leisure 1960–79
- **Key Topic 4:** Reasons for social change 1960–79

Zone in: how to get into the perfect 'zone' for revision.

Planning zone: tips and advice on how to plan revision effectively.

Know zone: the facts you need to know, memory tips and exam-style practice for every section.

Don't panic zone: last-minute revision tips.

Exam zone: what to expect on the exam paper.

Zone out: what happens after the exams.

Top Tips provide handy hints on how to apply what you have learned and how to remember key information and concepts.

examzone
Top tip

When considering the usefulness of a source, consider issues such as how representative or typical that view is. Also consider the nature of the source itself: some sources are more useful or reliable than others simply because of the type of source they are: a private report or letter is usually more reliable than a poster or tabloid newspaper. The usefulness of such sources depends on the question you need answers to!

The Know Zone Build better answers pages at the end of each section include a question with a student answer, comments and an improved answer so that you can see how to improve your own writing.

examzone
Build better answers

Question 2
Tip: this question will ask you to explain why a source was created – the purpose of the source. Some sources (for example a government report on education) might be created just to record what was happening. Others (such as a cartoon) might be created to get a message across and bring about a particular feeling or action in the reader. It is this second type of source that you will be asked about.

In this exam, there are several question types used to test this skill, for example 'Why do you think this poster was published?' or 'What was the purpose of this newspaper article?'

Let's use Source B on page 21 as our example and answer this question:

Why do you think this cartoon was published? (8 marks).

Student answer
There was a lot of racism at the time and the cartoonist shows how young people were the worst.

Comments
This is not a good response. It does identify a reason: 'shows how young people were the worst'. Though it gives a little bit of

---

Build better answers give you an opportunity to answer exam-style questions. They include tips for what a basic ■, good ● and excellent △ answer will contain.

examzone
Build better answers

Study Sources A, D, and E and use your own knowledge. Source D suggests that living conditions got worse in Britain in the 1950s. How far do you agree with this interpretation? Use your own knowledge, Sources A, D and E and any other sources you find helpful to explain your answer.
(16 marks)

■ **A basic answer (level 1)** a generalised answer without any specific support from the sources or own knowledge (for example, *I disagree with this interpretation because housing got better not worse*).

● **A good answer (level 2)** makes a judgement which agrees or disagrees with the interpretation and supports this with details from the sources and/or own knowledge (for example, ...the couple in Source C call their new flat a 'palace').

△ **A better answer (level 3)** answers at level 2, but then considers the degree to which support is provided. This could be by evaluating the sources' reliability (for example, Source A is clearly make living conditions sound better their supporters)

Unit 3: The source enquiry: an introduction

What is Unit 3 about?

The Unit 3 topics are very different from those in Units 1 and 2. To start with, you are never going to be asked just to recall historical information you have learned. If you find yourself sitting in an examination telling the story of what happened in a particular historical event, you are almost certainly not doing the right thing!

Unlike Units 1 and 2, Unit 3 is not about recalling or describing key features. Nor is it about using your knowledge to construct an argument about why things happened – or what the consequences of an action were. Instead, Unit 3 topics are about understanding the importance of sources in the study of history.

History as a subject is not just about learning a series of facts and repeating them in an examination. It is actually a process of enquiry. Historians understand that our historical knowledge comes from evidence from the past ('sources'). Historians have to piece together what has happened in the past from these sources. They need to interpret the sources to build up the historical picture. That is what you will be looking at in Unit 3.

Sources can sometimes be interpreted in a number of ways. They will also have been created for a variety of purposes. This means that historians also have to make judgements about the reliability of sources. You will learn ways of judging whether the information in a source is accurate or not. To make judgements about sources, you need to have some knowledge about the topic the sources relate to. You will need to use this information and the information in the sources to answer many of the questions in the examination. Don't tell the whole story, but select information from your own knowledge to support what you are saying about the source.

The examination

In the examination you will be given a collection of sources to study. Then you will be asked five questions. These five questions will test your understanding of interpreting sources. The good news is that each year the individual questions will always test the same skill. So Question 1 will always be about making an inference. The table at the top of the next page shows how this works.

Question	Marks	Type of question
1	6	Making inferences from sources
2	8	Considering the purpose of a source
3	10	Explaining causation using a source and own knowledge
4	10	Evaluating the reliability of sources
5	16	Evaluating a hypothesis
	+3	An additional 3 marks for spelling, punctuation and grammar are available in Question 5

So before you study the historical topic from which your sources will be drawn, let's make sure you know how to answer each question type. We have picked examples of sources from the Notting Hill Riots. You won't know the history yet, so you might want to read pages 20-21 before you go any further.

Making inferences from sources

When you read or look at a source and you understand its content, you are 'comprehending' that source. When you make a judgement from what the source says or shows, you are making an inference. Let us look at a source to see what that means.

Source A

Source A: From the Kensington News and West London Times, *5 September 1958*

I saw a mob of over 700 men, women and children stretching 200 yards along the road. Young children of ten were treating the whole affair as a great joke and shouting 'Come on, let's get the blacks and the coppers!' Women from the top floor windows laughed as they called down 'Go on boys, get yourself some blacks.'

This is how a journalist reported about the riot just after the event had taken place. In the examination, the sort of question you might be asked would be:

'What can you learn from Source A about why the Notting Hill riots happened?'

You could say: 'A mob of 700 men, women and children wanted to get the blacks.' That is true, but it doesn't take much working out, does it? It isn't an inference either, because that is exactly what the source says.

An inference that is definitely about the riots would be: 'I can learn that the riots were fuelled by widespread racism.' Can you see the difference? In the exam you would then want to prove the inference by adding: 'because the source tells me…'.

Considering the purpose of a source

It is important for historians to understand why sources have been created. Sometimes people are just recording what has happened (as in a diary), but sometimes a source is created to get a message across. For example, when a cartoonist sits down with a blank sheet of paper and draws a cartoon, he or she is doing so in order to get a message across. Let's look at an example.

| Source B | A cartoon published the day after one of the worst nights of violence in the Notting Hill riots. |

In the examination, the sort of question you might be asked about this source is:

'Why do you think this cartoon was published?'

You could say: *'because the Notting Hill riots were happening'*, but that is a very weak answer. A good answer would look at different details in the cartoon and work out why those have been drawn. The cartoon actually makes broader points rather than just focussing on racism. So the cartoonist wants to draw attention to the other, underlying causes of the riots (a lack of discipline in the young and understanding in the older generation). So the cartoonist wants to explain the causes of the riots – but for what purpose? The answer is to think more carefully about how young people are raised rather than just blaming them for the violence.

Explaining causation

Question 3 asks you to explain causation using a source and your own knowledge. Read this source.

| Source C | A character in Samuel Selvon's 1956 novel The Lonely Londoners *shares his experiences with a newly-arrived immigrant. Selvon himself was an immigrant from Trinidad.* |

'All right mister London, you been here a long time, what would you advice [sic] me as a newcomer to do?' 'I would advice you to go back home to Trinidad today'. When I was first here things used to go good enough. These days, spades all over the place and the English people don't like the boys coming to England to work and live.'
'Why is that?' Galahad ask.
'Well, they frighten that we get job in front of them, though that does never happen. The other thing is they just don't like black people.'

In the examination, the sort of question you might be asked is:

'Use Source C and your own knowledge to explain why the Notting Hill riots happened.'

Your task is to use the source and your own knowledge to explain why the Notting Hill riots happened. You must explain how the source shows this **and** add more from your own knowledge.

From the source you could extract: the post-war arrival of the 'Windrush generation'; the numbers of immigrants from the New Commonwealth by the mid-to late 1950s the racism faced by West Indian immigrants trying to find work. You will need to explain how these led to the Notting Hill riots, for example the 'Windrush generation' largely settled in a few poorer and cheaper areas of big cities such as Notting Hill in London. Now you need to add something from your own knowledge. You could add information about other areas where similar riots took place (e.g. St. Ann's in Nottingham or Handsworth in Birmingham) or the role of the government in encouraging immigration from the Caribbean (e.g. the British Nationality Act of 1948 that gave everyone in the Commonwealth the right to work and settle in Britain).

Evaluating the reliability of sources

Question 4 asks you consider how reliable two sources are as evidence of something. You must refer to both sources and use your own knowledge.

Let's look at Source A again. In the examination, the sort of question you might be asked is:

'How reliable is Source A as evidence about the Notting Hill riots?'

You could say: 'Source A was written by someone who interviewed people at the riots.' But this is just a general statement. To produce a good response you need to consider how likely the information is to be reliable, considering what you know about the situation. You also need to ask who has produced the source and why. These things affect reliability. The caption tells you it was a report on the riots for a local newspaper. The journalist is highly likely to have got several eye-witness statements. On the other hand, newspapers often exaggerate things to sell more copies. The detail about women laughing as they urged violence seems particularly shocking. It's very important to read the caption carefully and use all of the information it gives about the source.

Evaluating a hypothesis

Question 5 asks how far you agree with a statement. You will be expected to use some of the sources and your own knowledge to decide this. This is the sort of question you might be asked:

Source C suggests that the British were highly racist in the mid-1950s. How far do you agree with this interpretation?

The best answers make a judgement about how far they agree with the statement. They then provide detail from the sources **and** their own knowledge to support this judgement. For example: '...*Source A shows that it was not only Teddy Boys who held racist views but a broad section of men, women and children in the Notting Hill area and I know that in such areas it was acceptable for bed and breakfasts to put 'No blacks' signs in their windows.*

However, Source C shows that the British were usually not outwardly racist because of their polite 'diplomacy'. This suggests the British were not highly racist and that there were other reasons for the 'race riots' described in Source A.

Key Topic 1: British society and economy in the 1950s

Although the Second World War ended in 1945, its effects were felt well into the 1950s: rationing did not finally end until 1954 and bread rationing only began once the war had ended! Although a lot of war damage remained in many towns and cities, the most important change in post-war Britain was the gradual growth of prosperity after the hard years of Depression and war. Economic recovery and technological advances had many important consequences for the British people: more spending money for women and teenagers, more leisure time for men and new opportunities in Britain for black and South Asian citizens of the **British Commonwealth**. How would the British react to these new developments?

In this Key Topic you will study:

- the roles of men, women and children in the family in the 1950s
- the education system and approaches to the education of boys and girls in primary and secondary schools
- opportunities for leisure and popular leisure activities
- living and working conditions for men and women
- the reasons for and problems caused by immigration in the 1950s.

The British family in the 1950s

A British time-traveller from 1900 would feel far more at home with a family from the 1950s than one from our own time. Although things were already beginning to change, gender roles remained highly traditional, especially among the older generations:

- men went to work and were the 'bread-winners' for the family. Most men worked in manufacturing or heavy industry, as they had done in 1900
- women could do a limited range of jobs but were expected to stop work when they got married. While some of the jobs women did in the 1950s would have shocked a person from 1900, they would have recognised 'the **marriage bar**'
- children were expected to be respectful towards their elders and were punished if they failed to be so.

Although younger couples began to see marriage as more of an equal partnership, most married women were expected to do all the household chores. Many of the labour-saving domestic devices we take for granted today had not been invented or were unaffordable for most households, so housework was tiring and time-consuming. Divorce was difficult to obtain; while lots of couples overcame difficult periods, some were trapped in a loveless marriage. A family was very much expected to be a man, his wife and their children. With the exception of widowed single-parent families, anything other than this set up would have seemed very odd to British people in the 1950s.

| Source A | *A typical family scene from the 1950s* |

| Source B | *Doris Rich describes a typical weekday evening in a Midlands working-class family. Her account was published in 1953.* |

The evening starts when the men get home from work and all the family sit down to a cooked 'tea'. After eating, any youngsters (15 to 20s) wash, change clothes and go off to visit friends. At home the evening passes with the wife knitting or sewing and her husband playing with the children, resting and reading the newspapers. The wireless [radio] may be on in the background. At about 9pm the husband may go to his usual pub, leaving his wife to put the children to bed or continue with her knitting.

Activities

Look at Sources A and B.

1 Make a list of things in both sources that seem familiar to us today and things that seem different. Are there more differences or similarities?

2 Which source is more useful for finding out about British families in the 1950s? Why?

The education system

Learning objectives

In this chapter you will learn about:

- the education system in the 1950s
- approaches to the education of boys and girls in primary and secondary schools.

Towards the end of the Second World War the government introduced the 1944 Education Act. Its authors hoped to replace the hotchpotch of different schools that existed before the war with a national system that ensured a proper education for all. These changes affected the lives of 95 per cent of all school pupils in the 1950s.

Activity

1 Look at Source A. How far would you have supported the recommendations of the 1944 Education Act? Have a class debate on the possible advantages and disadvantages of the new system.

Source A *A diagram showing the tripartite system of schooling.*

Primary School
- For ages 5–11
- Infants aged 5–7; juniors ages 7–11
- Mixed-sex classes
- Classes divided by ability

Secondary Technical Schools
- Specialised in mechanical and technical education
- Very few established due to high cost

Secondary Modern Schools
- Provided a general, all-round education
- 70 per cent of pupils went here in 1950s
- Pupils left at 15 with a Certificate of Education
- Some pupils went on to Technical College for more vocational training
- Over half were mixed-sex

Grammar Schools
- Provided a highly academic education including subjects such as Classics and Latin.
- 20 per cent of pupils went here in 1950s
- Most pupils stayed until aged 16 to take O-level exams
- Many went on to take A-levels and then to university
- Mainly single-sex schools.

The Eleven Plus and the tripartite system

At the heart of the 1944 Act was the Eleven Plus exam, so-called because pupils took it at the end of junior school at age eleven. The exam decided which type of secondary school was 'most suitable' for each pupil. Source A shows how the tripartite (three parts) system operated in most of England and Wales until the early 1970s.

The authors of the 1944 Act hoped that a '**parity of esteem**' would exist between pupils leaving the different types of school. In reality, the extra funding enjoyed by grammar schools, together with the lack of technical schools, meant that the Eleven Plus came to be seen as a pass/fail test with those who failed the test condemned to what was regarded as an inferior education at secondary moderns.

The Curriculum

For both boys and girls at junior schools, morning lessons focused on literacy and numeracy with a range of broad subjects later in the day. Boys and girls continued to do similar core subjects at grammar or secondary modern schools, although there were some differences: girls took subjects such as needlework, home economics and sometimes 'mothercraft', while boys did woodwork and metalwork. These differences clearly reflected the different expectations of boys' and girls' paths upon leaving school: boys would find a career, while girls would soon settle to marriage and motherhood.

Source B	A photo of a class at Forefield Junior School in the 1950s. Those who did well in the frequent tests sat nearer the front of the class.

Source C	From the poet Michael Rosen's blog in July 2012. Here he remembers his experiences of junior school in the 1950s

Every day was laced with 11-plus-ness. That's to say, Miss Williams was constantly warning those of us in the middle of the class that we could fail and would have to go to a secondary modern school. I remember her standing in the middle of the class and holding out her arms telling us that everyone on 'this' side would pass and everyone on 'that' side would fail.

Source D	A modern historian discusses working-class attitudes to boys' and girls' education in the 1950s

The value of education was seen as particularly low for daughters; but either way, whether a son or a daughter, at a grammar or a secondary modern, the pressure was almost always on to leave as early as possible and get a job.

Activities

1 How surprising do you find Source D?

2 Did you sit the Eleven Plus? If you didn't, ask a parent or grandparent, if possible, about their experiences of school; do they remember the Eleven Plus? If not, there are lots of memoirs online.

examzone
Build better answers

Study Source C. What can you learn from Source C about the education system in the 1950s? (6 marks)

■ **A basic answer (level 1)** just repeats information in the source (for example, *we learn that if pupils failed the eleven plus they had to go to secondary modern schools*).

● **A good answer (level 2)** makes an inference but does not support it from the source (for example, *we learn that passing the eleven plus was very important for some pupils and teachers*).

▲ **An excellent answer (level 3)** makes three inferences and supports them from the source (for example, *...because the teacher issued 'constant' warnings and the pupil still remembers the '11-plus-ness' of the lessons over 50 years later*).

Did you know?

Scotland has had a separate education system since the founding of the first schools in Britain after the Reformation in the 16th century; the changes discussed on this page only affected England, Wales and, to a lesser degree, Northern Ireland (which adopted a similar tripartite system to England and Wales after 1947).

Popular leisure activities

Learning objectives

In this chapter you will learn about:
- opportunities for leisure in the 1950s
- popular leisure activities In the 1950s.

Opportunities

Men and women, especially among the working classes, had fewer opportunities for leisure activities in the 1950s than later generations enjoyed. This was due to two things:

- **Time**: men worked on average 40 minutes longer per day and had 2 weeks less holiday per year in the 1950s than by 1979 (and this was after a 1948 Act of Parliament had doubled annual paid holiday to two weeks!). By 1979 women spent at least 30 minutes less on housework per day. This was largely due to the rise in ownership of labour-saving devices like vacuum cleaners, but men also began to do a lot more housework.

- **Disposable income**: in 1953, a man's average wage would cover a weekly food bill after 15 hours' work; by 1981 this had fallen to 9 hours. The rise in the numbers of women in work further increased a family's disposable income.

Popular activities

Some things in British life have changed little: then, as now, sports such as football and hobbies such as gardening and fishing were highly popular with men of different ages. According to their age, women enjoyed domestic craft hobbies, bingo, dance, swimming (at lidos) and tennis, but had fewer opportunities to participate in team sports, which were still generally thought to be 'unfeminine'.

Source A | A photo of a British family watching television in the mid-1950s

About two-thirds of people's leisure time is currently spent in the home. This would have been slightly less in the 1950s, in the main due to the lack of modern entertainment technology: almost every home had a radio but very few had a television in the early 1950s. Television ownership took off after Queen Elizabeth's coronation in 1953. Just 15,000 TV licences were issued in 1947; this had risen to 10.5 million by 1960! Far more people enjoyed regular public viewing of sport or films than today.

- There were just under 40 million admissions to football matches in England in 1950; despite a large population increase this has fallen to around 25 million admissions today
- There were 1.4 billion cinema admissions per year in 1950, a figure that had already fallen to 515 million by 1959. Children especially loved Saturday morning cinema where cartoons, comedies and adventure films were screened.

Then, as now, summer was the time to take holidays. In the 1950s less than 2 per cent took overseas holidays; the majority went to the seaside by coach or train. Many factories would close for what was known as 'Wakes Week' in many towns; the whole town could feel deserted as workers went to the seaside. This was not very different from the way in which holidays had been taken by the majority of people from the late 19th century onwards. The latest craze, particularly among working-class families, was to take a holiday at one of the new holiday camps. With the rise in disposable income these were much more affordable and many poorer families were able to go away on holiday for the first time.

Source B *Author Valerie Tedder remembers what it was like staying in holiday camps in the 1950s, from her 1999 book* Post-War Blues.

We made use of the baby listening service a couple of times. All you had to do to let staff know there was a baby sleeping inside the chalet, was to tie a large white handkerchief on the door knob. Any child heard crying was reported by the staff on patrol and the message was given out over the tannoy system in the ballroom, 'Baby crying in chalet number…' It was noticeable that many fathers did the honours, leaving the mothers to enjoy the evening undisturbed. At the end of the evening the entertainment ended with the singing of the National Anthem. Loud noise and shouting was banned.

examzone

Build better answers

Study Source C and use your own knowledge. What was the purpose of the poster shown as Source C? Use details from the source and your own knowledge to explain your answer. **(8 marks)**

■ **A basic answer (level 1)** gives a reason why the poster was made but does not use details of the source or knowledge to back up the answer.

● **A good answer (level 2)** gives a reason why the poster was made (to encourage families to take their holiday at the holiday camp) and uses details of the source **or** own knowledge to explain the purpose of the source.

▲ **An excellent answer (level 3)** gives a reason why the poster was made and uses details from the source **and** own knowledge to explain the purpose of the source (to appeal to different genders' typical interests, to take advantage of recent increases in annual paid holiday and take business away from seaside hotels).

Popular leisure activities

13

Activities

1 How reliable is Source A as evidence of popular leisure activities in the 1950s?

2 In what ways might the rapid growth of television ownership in the 1950s have affected other popular leisure activities?

Source C *An advert for a Butlin's holiday camp from the 1950s.*

Living and working conditions

Learning objectives

In this chapter you will learn about:
- rates of pay and working conditions for men
- living conditions in the 1950s.

Never had it so good? Work and pay

Very few people have suffered **absolute poverty** in Britain since the Second World War. Instead there have been different degrees of relative poverty: people compare themselves to others to judge how well-off they are. From our perspective most people in the 1950s appear poor. However, compared to the tough times before and during the war, many people in the 1950s enjoyed the benefits of the new **welfare state** and the post-war economic **boom**. Britain enjoyed **full employment** in the 1950s; men's wages rose faster than prices until the government tried to stop **inflation** by limiting wage increases.

Source A	The actor Albert Finney as the working class anti-hero Arthur Seaton in the 1960 film Saturday Night and Sunday Morning. *The character worked long hours at the Raleigh factory in Nottingham to earn money to spend on clothes, beer and cigarettes.*

Source B	Conservative Prime Minister Harold Macmillan gives his view of the British quality of life at a Party rally in July 1957.

Most of our people have never had it so good. Go around the country, go to the industrial towns, go to the farms and you will see a state of prosperity such as we have never had in my lifetime – nor indeed in the history of this country.

Source C	A table that compares what an average working-class man in Sheffield could buy with a week's pay in 1950 and in 2007.

	1950	2007
Percentage of a house	0.61	0.020
Percentage of a car	1.0	2.7
Packs of cigarettes	43	48
Litres of petrol	182	277
Cinema tickets	31	49
Mars bars	122	747
Tram journeys	305	153
Pints of beer	76	107

Activities

1 Look at Source C. Which items have become relatively cheaper and which more expensive? Are you surprised by any of the changes listed in the source?

2 'Source A is almost worthless for finding out about men's working conditions in the late 1950s' How far do you agree?

Never had it so good? Living conditions

Many people lived in inadequate houses before the war, but a huge programme of slum-clearance and house-building before and after the war meant many more people had homes with adequate heating, an indoor toilet and hot and cold running water. The biggest change for people in many towns and cities was the post-war construction of blocks of flats to house people who had lived in urban slums.

Source D	Gladys Langford, a teacher from Islington who kept a diary from 1936-69, records her views on changes in Hackney, East London in the early 1950s.

It was a most attractive spot with trees and pleasing views. Now huge blocks of flats and ugly little shops scar the mangled roads. Two of the blocks with grey stone look like Pentonville Prison. There is nothing attractive left. I am sure the character of the residents of London must be adversely affected by such hideous communal life. Poor old London!

Source E	From a 1961 short film about a young family settling into their home in Glasgow's Mossheight flats.

In this house, with all its modern facilities, a mother can care for her children as she always wanted to. She's no longer concerned that they are breathing germs and disease in a refuse littered back court. When they come in from play she has hot water on tap to wash away the healthy dirt they have collected. Later, the children will go to bed in their own rooms.

examzone

Build better answers

Study Sources B, D and E and use your own knowledge. Source D suggests that living conditions got worse in Britain in the 1950s. How far do you agree with this interpretation? Use your own knowledge, Sources B, D and E and any other sources you find helpful to explain your answer.

(16 marks)

■ **A basic answer (level 1)** a generalised answer without any specific support from the sources or own knowledge (for example, *I disagree with this interpretation because housing got better not worse*).

● **A good answer (level 2)** makes a judgement which agrees **or** disagrees with the interpretation and supports this with details from the sources and/or own knowledge (for example, ... *Source E says the new houses have moved children away from 'a refuse littered back court' and that they now have 'their own rooms'*.

▲ **A better answer (level 3)** answers at level 2, but then considers the degree to which support is provided. This could be by evaluating the sources' reliability (for example, *Source B is clearly trying to make living conditions sound better to impress their supporters*).

▲ **An excellent answer (level 4)** answers at level 3 but considers both sides of the argument before reaching a balanced judgement. You **must** use own knowledge to achieve level 4!

Make sure you write accurately when answering these questions - there are 3 extra marks available for spelling, grammar and punctuation.

Did you know?

In 1951:

10 per cent of British homes lacked electricity.

25 per cent did not have an indoor toilet

33 per cent had an iron tub instead of a fixed bath

Women's work

Learning objectives

In this chapter you will learn about:
- popular attitudes to women in work
- rates of pay and working conditions for the average working woman.

Popular attitudes

Gender inequality in the workplace still makes the news today.

Activities

1 Even today, British women are on average paid less and promoted less often to senior roles than men. Why do you think this is? Is it fair?

2 Is it a good thing that many mothers with young children can go to work today? Discuss your views with the class and note arguments for and against.

The issues you have just discussed also caused debate in the 1950s, although it would have been 'married women' instead of 'mothers with young children' in question. While a lot of married women were content in their role as housewives, many others were bored with being stuck at home. Perhaps it was the experience of work during the Second World War that fuelled a desire to work: many women had enjoyed making new friends and finding fulfilment outside the home. While most men had traditional views on a woman's place, some younger men were supportive of their wives working until childbirth. Working-class women would often return to work when their children were old enough to look after themselves but too young to earn a wage.

Did you know?

Until the 1970s a married women needed her husband's signature to get a credit card, mortgage or bank loan.

Source A — From Women and Families, An Oral History 1940-70, *by social historian Elizabeth Roberts, published in 1995.*

Working women's views were that while it was desirable to earn money, it was not right to have a job with long hours that would leave them too tired to care for their families. Besides, who was to look after the children? Women did not complain about low wages – particularly low compared to those of her husband. Women's wages were seen as being for 'extras' while men's wages were for essentials.

Source B — Extracts from **Mass Observation** *interviews with 644 married men in 1957.*

When a woman goes out to work, the home soon falls apart. (Metalworker, aged 39)

Working women are one of the main causes of child delinquency. (Engineer, aged 47)

Source C — A table showing the percentages of women in the British workforce, 1951–81.

	1951	1961	1971	1981
Percentage of workforce that are women	31	33	37	40
Percentage of 20–64-year-old women in workforce	36	42	52	61
Percentage of 20–64-year-old women employed part-time	12	26	35	42
Percentage of married women in the workforce	26	35	49	62

Work and pay for women

For women who wanted fair pay and a fair opportunity to work and win promotion, there were considerable obstacles to overcome:

- most working-class girls left school at 15 with no qualifications. Girls who did stay on to 16 often went to college to study in areas such as secretarial skills, childcare, or hairdressing. One in four women in work were secretaries in the late 1950s.

- few women went to university. In the early 1960s, women made up only a quarter of undergraduate students. Very few women studied science, engineering, medicine or law. Only 15 per cent of doctors and 5 per cent of the law profession were women.

- nearly a third of all women were still teenagers when they got married. Nine times as many women as men were married before the age of 19 and the average age of getting married was 22 years old.

- most women gave birth to their first child in the first three years of marriage: almost two thirds of all births were to women under the age of 25. It was not acceptable for mothers with young children to work; employers argued that women returning to work would be unwilling to work long hours and would need to take time off work if their children were ill.

- women's magazines often reinforced traditional social attitudes (including those to female work) with messages such as 'happy family', 'keeping your man', and 'be more beautiful'.

- most jobs were still in traditionally male areas of industry and manufacturing.

- there were no laws enforcing equal pay or opportunities for women.

Nevertheless, the number of women in work, especially part-time work, did gradually increase. The range of jobs they did remained quite limited, and limiting!

Source D A magazine aimed at women from June 1953. The articles include knitting patterns for children's clothes and cake decorating tips.

Exam-style question

1 What can you learn from Source A about women and work in the 1950s? (6 marks)

2 How reliable are Sources B and D as evidence of popular attitudes to women's work in the 1950s? (10 marks)

examzone
Top tip

When considering the usefulness of a source, consider issues such as how representative or typical that view is. Also consider the nature of the source itself: some sources are more useful or reliable than others simply because of the type of source they are: a private report or letter is usually more reliable than a poster or tabloid newspaper. The usefulness of such sources depends on the question you need answers to!

Immigration: *Windrush* and beyond

Learning objectives

In this chapter you will learn about:
- the reasons for Commonwealth immigration
- the stories of the 'Windrush generation'.

What was so special about the *Windrush* generation?

The most numerous group of migrants into Britain by the late 1950s were the Irish: over 900,000 Irish people had settled in Britain by 1959, compared with only 200,000 people from the **New Commonwealth**. Yet it was not these Irish immigrants who were chosen to feature prominently in the 2012 Olympic Games opening ceremony. Instead it was the 492 West Indians who arrived on the SS *Empire Windrush* in June 1948 who were chosen.

Source A *A representation of the arrival in Britain on 22 June 1948 of the* Empire Windrush *at the 2012 Olympic Games opening ceremony.*

Activity

1 At the opening ceremony, director Danny Boyle put on a show that he hoped would help the rest of the world understand modern Britain, and what it means to be British. Why do you think he chose to give such prominence to the 'Windrush generation'? Do you think he was justified in doing so? You might want to revisit this question later in the course!

Why was there so much immigration into Britain in the 1950s?

There was a range of push and pull factors that help to explain immigration from the New Commonwealth in the 1950s:

- **Shortage of labour:** Britain enjoyed full employment because of the post-war economic boom. In fact, there were not enough British workers to fill all the available positions, especially low-paid and unskilled jobs.

- **Law:** The 1948 British Nationality Act made all people living in the Commonwealth British citizens. This gave them the right to travel to Britain without a visa and to settle there if they wished. The law was not changed until 1962, by which time over half a million black and South Asian people had settled in Britain.

- **Recruitment campaigns by British firms:** The National Health Service (only set up in 1948), textile firms in northern England and London Transport advertised available jobs in the New Commonwealth. London Transport even sent representatives to the Caribbean to search for staff: 140 men were recruited in Barbados in 1956 alone. Black men from the Caribbean became a familiar sight on London buses as drivers and conductors in the 1950s.

- **Immigrant ambitions and views of Britain:** Many saw working in Britain, the 'mother country', as an opportunity to earn good wages. Many had been to Britain during their time in the armed forces in the Second World War and found the West Indian islands 'too small' when they went home. Most earlier immigrants were male and aimed to work in Britain for a short period while sending money back to their families, before returning back 'home' themselves. Many later immigrants settled and then encouraged their families to join them in Britain.

- **Encouragement and support for immigrants:** Some immigrants were given an interest-free loan from their own government for travel costs. London Transport provided hostels for many of the immigrants it recruited.

Passengers on-board the Empire Windrush *catch up on the latest news in the Jamaican newspaper* The Daily Gleaner *shortly before their arrival at Tilbury Docks in London on 22 June 1948.*

The Windrush generation

The SS *Empire Windrush* docked at Tilbury docks in London on 22 June 1948. A few already had jobs lined up with London Transport, but for many others the future was uncertain. Many men spent their first few days in canvas tents at a camp set up especially for them in Clapham, South London. Here they received free food and shelter while they found work and more permanent lodgings. From here, many men moved to nearby Brixton where they found cheap lodgings.

Many Londoners would only see the West Indian men driving buses, or perhaps as entertainers in a few central music venues. Their arrival caused quite a stir, especially in the areas where they settled; this was partly due to their 'exotic' accents and music, but largely because of the colour of their skin. The men faced a good deal of racial prejudice.

Clinton Edwards, a passenger on the Empire Windrush, *remembers his experiences in an interview for the BBC in 1998.*

I first came to England during the war, in the RAF. When I went back home there was no work so I decided to come back. There was a boat coming back, by the name of *Windrush* and it was only £28, so I paid my fare and come back. When I came back it was a bit more difficult. I was a civilian then, I had to find work. The first job I got as a welder, instead of doing welding they gave me a wheelbarrow and a shovel. After a couple of weeks my arms (laughter) were sore. So I packed it in and re-enlisted in the RAF.

Activities

2 Look at the push and pull factors leading to immigration in the 1950s. Would you say that there were more push or pull factors that explain post-war immigration? Make a table with two columns and sort the causes into push and pull factors.

3 What would you argue was the most important cause of post-war immigration from the New Commonwealth? Why?

4 Look at sources A, B and C. Which source would be of most use to an historian who wants to learn about the arrival of the *Windrush* generation? Explain your answer!

Riots and racism

Learning objectives

In this chapter you will learn about:

● the extent of racism in parts of Britain and in popular culture

● the Notting Hill riots and other race-related riots in the 1950s.

Welcome to Britain?

For many immigrants, Britain was not as welcoming as they had expected. Those migrating to Britain arrived with little money and so logically sought accommodation in the cheapest areas of towns and cities. Some of these areas, such as St Ann's in Nottingham, Toxteth in Liverpool, Handsworth in Birmingham and Brixton in London, attracted so many immigrants that the original white population began to move out to other parts of the city. By 1957 the government was concerned at what was described as 'white-flight' and 'segregation' in some of Britain's major towns and cities. Tensions started to develop within these mainly white working-class communities:

● Some trade unions complained about immigrants taking jobs from whites by accepting work at lower wages.

● Some young men, especially those in working-class '**Teddy Boy**' gangs, sought to intimidate black men who were 'taking their women'.

● Some politicians argued that, instead of coming to Britain to work, many were coming to Britain simply to receive generous welfare benefits.

● 'No coloureds' and 'No blacks' could often be seen on signs for accommodation or in advertisements for job vacancies. Many black immigrants were forced to take overcrowded and substandard accommodation.

As the black immigrants were overwhelmingly young men, they did like to drink, dance and flirt. However, sensationalised reports in newspapers about the supposed lack of cleanliness, criminal activities and sexual practices of recent immigrants blamed their behaviour, not on their social and financial circumstances, but on their race.

Source A

A sign reading 'no Irish, no blacks, no dogs' displayed in a British guest house window in the early 1960s.

A number of films in the late 1950s also depicted black people in a racist fashion that helped to reinforce stereotypical prejudice.

The Notting Hill Race Riots

In the St Ann's area of Nottingham almost 1,000 white and black youths fought each other on the night of 23 August 1958; a number of stabbings occurred. These were followed by riots in Notting Hill, London. The riot was sparked by the attack on a white woman with a black partner by a gang of Teddy Boys. Over a period of almost two weeks in August and September, the riot escalated, with hundreds of young, white men armed with chains, knives, iron bars and petrol bombs attacking groups of black immigrants and their homes with chants such as 'niggers out'. More than a hundred white men were arrested as well as some black men who had armed themselves in self-defence. The riots received widespread news coverage both within Britain and internationally. The Notting Hill Carnival was founded the following year to promote racial harmony.

Source B | *A cartoon published the day after one of the worst nights of violence in the Notting Hill riots.*

Source C | *From the Kensington News and West London Times, 5 September 1958*

I saw a mob of over 700 men, women and children stretching 200 yards along the road. Young children of ten were treating the whole affair as a great joke and shouting 'Come on, let's get the blacks and the coppers!' Women from the top floor windows laughed as they called down 'Go on boys, get yourself some blacks.'

Source D | *A character in Samuel Selvon's 1956 novel* The Lonely Londoners *shares his experiences with a newly-arrived immigrant. Selvon himself was an immigrant from Trinidad.*

'All right mister London, you been here a long time, what would you advice [sic] me as a newcomer to do?'
'I would advice you to go back home to Trinidad today'. When I was first here things used to go good enough. These days, spades [black people] all over the place and the English people don't like the boys coming to England to work and live.'
'Why is that?' Galahad ask.
'Well, they frighten that we get job in front of them, though that does never happen. The other thing is they just don't like black people.'

Exam-style question

Study Sources B, C and D and use your own knowledge. Source D suggests that the British were largely racist in the 1950s. How far do you agree with this interpretation? Use your own knowledge, Sources B, C and D and any other sources you find helpful to explain your answer. (16 marks)

Overall, British public opinion was shocked by the events at Notting Hill. Much of the British public had seen television news coverage of the police trying to keep black and white groups apart, and fire-fighters putting out fires caused by petrol bombs being thrown. In some ways the Notting Hill riots were a turning point:

- There was some resentment and anger from the black community as many felt that at the time the police purposely downplayed the racial element of the riots.
- After the Notting Hill riots more than 4,000 immigrants (around 3 per cent of the total immigrant population) returned to the Caribbean.
- An official complaint was made by Caribbean governments to the British government; they were particularly concerned about prejudiced policing and the effects of poor housing.
- Both political and public opinion became divided. *The Times* commented on 'the ugliest fighting' whereas the *Daily Mail* asked its readers 'Should we let them carry on coming in?'
- Immigrant groups in Britain became more organised. The Organisation for the Protection of Coloured People was set up. There was also, for example, a rent strike in Notting Hill by some immigrants until repairs were carried out on their housing.

There then began a series of debates about the extent of immigration to British inner cities and how to deal with racial tension and racism. At national government level, policies on immigration had to start to address two main issues:

- the numbers of immigrants entering Britain
- methods to tackle racial discrimination.

Activities

1 Create a short story that captures the reasons for and impact of the Notting Hill riots, either from the perspective of a Teddy Boy or from that of a recently arrived black immigrant.

2 Has racism disappeared from British society and culture today? Are things as bad today as in the 1950s? Discuss these issues as a class and think about the reasons for continuity or change in levels of racism.

22

In the Unit 3 examination, you will be required to answer five questions, applying your skills of source analysis to six sources on a topic from the Modern World Source Enquiry you have studied.

You only have one hour and 15 minutes to answer these questions, so the examiners are not expecting you to write huge amounts. The number of marks helps you judge how much to write. The time allocation below gives a little thinking time before you

put pen to paper and a few minutes to read through your answers at the end.

Question 1: 10 minutes

Question 2: 12 minutes

Question 3: 12 minutes

Question 4: 12 minutes

Question 5: 20 minutes

Here, we are going to look at Questions 1 and 2.

examzone
Build better answers

Question 1

Tip: Question 1 will ask you to make an inference from a source and provide evidence from the source to support it. Let's look at an example.

Source B *From a 1961 short film about a young family settling into their home in Glasgow's Mossheight flats.*

In this house, with all its modern facilities, a mother can care for her children as she always wanted to. She's no longer concerned that they are breathing germs and disease in a refuse littered back court. When they come in from play she has hot water on tap to wash away the healthy dirt they have collected. Later, the children will go to bed in their own rooms.

What can you learn from Source B about living conditions in Britain in the 1960s? (6 marks)

Student answer	Comment
This source tells me that some people had 'hot water on tap'. People must have found the new flats healthier than their old houses.	The first part of this answer merely repeats information contained in the source, so it would be marked at level 1. The last sentence does make an inference (a judgement which is not actually stated in the source) when it says that the new housing led to healthier living conditions in the 1960s. However, it does not say what in the source makes it possible to make that inference; it is therefore an unsupported inference marked at level 2 rather than level 3. Let's re-write the answer with that additional detail.
This source tells me that the quality of housing improved in the 1960s in terms of living space and hygiene. You can tell this because the family have more than one bedroom in the new flat and have hot running water for the first time. The source also suggests that living conditions were worse for people in areas with older housing because of the cramped conditions, lack of 'modern facilities' and the amount of rubbish in the back alleys.	An inference made and well supported, so it's a level 3 answer. Another supported inference or two would have led to a more complete answer.

examzone

Build better answers

Question 2

Tip: this question will ask you to explain why a source was created – the purpose of the source. Some sources (for example a government report on education) might be created just to record what was happening. Others (such as a cartoon) might be created to get a message across and bring about a particular feeling or action in the reader. It is this second type of source that you will be asked about.

In this exam, there are several question types used to test this skill, for example 'Why do you think this poster was published?' or 'What was the purpose of this newspaper article?'

Let's use Source B on page 21 as our example and answer this question:

Why do you think this cartoon was published? (8 marks).

Student answer	Comments
There was a lot of racism at the time and the cartoonist shows how young people were the worst.	This is not a good response. It does identify a reason: 'shows how young people were the worst'. Though it gives a little bit of context: 'there was a lot of racism at the time', there is no explanation linking the message to the historical context in any meaningful way. Let's rewrite the answer to provide the detail.
The cartoonist wants something to be done to prevent the kind of racist violence seen in race riots of 1958. Thousands of young men, especially those in Teddy Boy gangs, took part in violent clashes against black people who had recently moved into areas such as St. Ann's in Nottingham and Notting Hill in London. The Teddy Boy is clearly shown with his long coat, drainpipe trousers and quiff haircut; the violence he plans is shown by the knife and broken bottle in his hands. The expression of his father shows the feelings of shock and lack of understanding that most British people felt when they heard about the riots. The cartoonist seems to suggest that more discipline is needed: older methods such as use of the belt or cane might have stopped such violence.	This is a big improvement. The message ('something needs to be done about racist violence') is explained and supported well. That would be marked at level 2. But the answer then moves from the message to the purpose (to encourage older forms of discipline for young offenders). That makes this a level 3 answer.

Key Topic 2: Education, work and labour relations 1960–79

The generation of politicians after the Second World War had hoped to build a better Britain for all. In some ways they made incredible advances in a time of general shortage. However, for a number of reasons, some of which were beyond the government's control, division and dissent began to emerge in British society in the 1960s and especially 1970s. What had changed? Why did a time of purpose, progress and prosperity give way to a period of stagnation and a feeling that Britain had become the 'sick man of Europe'?

In this Key Topic you will study:

- the increasing backlash against the tripartite education system and the Eleven Plus exam
- the extent of change in education and the rise of the comprehensive school 1960–79
- changes in employment and the causes of increased unemployment in the 1970s
- the impact of the 1973 oil crisis on the British people
- labour relations: the three-day week, 1974 miners' strike and 1979 'Winter of Discontent'.

The comprehensive experiment

Learning objectives

In this chapter you will learn about:
- the different experiences of education at grammar and secondary modern schools
- the backlash against the Eleven Plus exam and the rise of comprehensive schools.

What's the point of education?

Education was (and remains) a highly divisive issue: should schools be traditional institutions that promote discipline and the acquisition of knowledge or should they be more **progressive** and promote key skills like group-work and self-motivated learning? Above all, politicians, parents and students have argued about the main purpose of education: should it promote competition and maximise individual progress or should it promote cooperation and greater social equality?

Activity

Which of the viewpoints above would you most support? Consider your views and then have a class debate.

Between 1960 and 1979, the debate centred on whether comprehensive schools should replace the tripartite system that divided students between grammar, technical and secondary modern schools, based on their ability. Some **LEA**s had rejected the tripartite system from the start (they were able to do this because they had a great deal of **autonomy**: central government only intervened directly in a few matters). By 1964, 10 per cent of pupils went to comprehensive schools that took pupils of all ability. In 1965, the Labour Education Secretary, Anthony Crosland, issued a document (called circular 10/65) that called for universal comprehensive education.

Source A *From Anthony Crosland's circular 10/65*

It is the Government's aim to end selection at eleven plus and to eliminate separatism in secondary education...The Secretary of State requests LEAs, if they have not already done so, to prepare plans for reorganising secondary education in their areas on comprehensive lines...The spontaneous and exciting progress which has been made in this direction by so many LEAs in recent years demonstrates that the objective is not only achievable; it is also now widely accepted. The Government believes that both the education service and the general public will welcome the further change.

Exam-style question

What can you learn from Source A about education in England and Wales in the 1960s? (6 marks)

To reform or not reform?

There were arguments for and against such reform and many LEAs looked as if they might ignore circular 10/65. In 1966 the government issued another document that said funding for new schools or school refurbishment would only go to LEAs that adopted comprehensive reform; this financial pressure led many LEAs to feel forced to adopt the new system.

Arguments for comprehensive education	Arguments against comprehensive education
Grammar schools on average had three times the resources of secondary modern schools. This did not promote 'parity' as promised in the 1944 Education Act.	Many grammar schools were excellent and produced highly successful students.
Many secondary modern schools were already run-down by the 1960s; many children would avoid such poor schools with comprehensive reform.	Grammar schools were seen as a precious opportunity for social advancement by many working-class families with bright children.
Pupils who failed the eleven-plus were condemned to a life of fewer opportunities: only two per cent of those who failed the exam were still in school at the age of 17.	In 1975, the government forced **direct grant grammar** schools to go comprehensive. Many went independent instead; free places were removed and poorer local parents could not afford the fees.
The eleven-plus favoured middle-class over working-class children: very few children from working-class areas passed the exam.	The rise of more private schools in place of grammar schools led to a system that promoted less social equality.
The majority of the public wanted to scrap the eleven-plus.	The majority of the public wanted to keep grammar schools.

Momentum for comprehensive education built throughout the 1960s and 70s. Teachers' unions and middle-class parents (who feared their children going to secondary moderns if they failed the eleven-plus) were especially vocal in their support for comprehensive reform.

Labour continued to support the idea of comprehensive education throughout the 1970s. In 1976 Labour Prime Minister, James Callaghan, made clear his party's position in a speech, emphasising free and comprehensive education for all. That same year his government had passed the 1976 Education Act, clearly showing the principle for education should not be based on selection, by the eleven-plus or otherwise.

Source B	Percentage of students at comprehensive schools
1970	33
1974	62
1979	90

Source C Details from a Labour Party election pamphlet from 1964.

What about the grammar schools?

What about the grammar schools?

Labour will not do away with grammar education or abolish the best traditions of this type of education.

Labour's aim is to greatly increase the opportunities for children to receive the undoubted benefits of grammar education.

Labour is determined to open the door of opportunity to all children. To do this, the next Labour Government will require local education authorities to submit plans designed to adopt the comprehensive principle of education as quickly as possible.

Comprehensive education does not mean that the virtues of the grammar school are destroyed. They will be extended to a wider group of children whose talents will be enriched by the higher standards created for all by the comprehensive system.

At the same time they will grow up in school with children of differing talents – the future scientist, office worker, technician, the 'tinker and the tailor' of the modern world will learn, at an early age, to live together.

The Conservative government of 1970–74 did little to stop the reform, but throughout the 1970s increasingly vocal opposition to comprehensive education started to grow. Criticism of the system, supported by several right-leaning newspapers, focussed on what was seen as a lack of support for more intellectually gifted, high-achieving pupils. They also criticised what they saw as a lack of discipline in the classroom.

The newly-elected Conservative government of 1979 responded and repealed Labour's 1976 Education Act, meaning the government and LEAs were no longer obliged to follow the principle of 'no selection', but by that time there were only 150 grammar schools left.

Source D	A former Head Boy writes in a local newspaper on the closure of his grammar school in 1973.

Impressions of the school still fill the mind. In my last year I remember sitting for a Cambridge scholarship in the room of the headmistress and feeling, as she fussed to make sure that everything was in order and I was fully at ease, that she would have taken the papers for me had she been allowed. Maybe the time has come for the school to die, as education in this country enters a new stage. But if what Eccles Grammar School stood for in education dies then something very valuable will have died in England.

Source E	Catriona Nicholson, writing in 2013, remembers her time at a Secondary Modern School.

For five years I was a pupil at a run-down Secondary Modern School. The first three years of that schooling were grim and dispiriting ones. We, being eleven-plus 'failures', disrupted teachers' attempts at pupil control whenever we could. The effect of that sense of not measuring up to expectations left me mute, mulish and deeply hesitant. Then a new Head arrived and in his enthusiastic wake came a distinctive uniform, a school badge with a motto, a new curriculum, the opportunity to sit national exams, refurbished classrooms, new books etc. But for my class, the most joyous and momentous thing of all was the appointment of our new teacher. He was a Cambridge graduate whose beliefs in how Secondary Modern kids could achieve, led him to our ailing school and our classroom.

Did you know?

During her time as Conservative Minister for Education (1970–74), Margaret Thatcher approved more conversions of grammar schools to comprehensives than any other Education minister.

Activities

1 Look at the arguments for and against comprehensive reform. Which side of the argument do you find the more persuasive? Why?

2 Study Sources D and E. How far do they support the arguments for or against comprehensive reform?

3 How reliable are Sources D and E as evidence of pupils' experiences of education in England and Wales before major comprehensive reform?

Exam-style question

Use Source C and your own knowledge to explain why comprehensive reform rapidly increased in England and Wales after 1964. (10 marks)

The battle for education

> **Learning objectives**
>
> In this chapter you will learn about:
> - the challenge of 'progressive' ideas in education
> - the impact of educational changes on pupils.

Progressive education

Although LEAs enjoyed their autonomy, they did not have the powers to control headteachers and teachers who wanted to teach differently in their schools. As a result there were sometimes large variations in the way pupils were taught at different schools. Many teachers began to introduce the progressive reforms that had been championed in the 1967 Plowden Report on primary schools. The report recommended a more 'child-centred' approach to education.

Source A	From the 1967 Plowden Report, produced by the educational reformer Lady Plowden.

A school is not merely a teaching shop, it must transmit values and attitudes. It is a community in which children learn to live first and foremost as children and not as future adults. The school sets out deliberately to devise the right environment for children, to allow them to be themselves and to develop in the way and at the pace appropriate to them. It lays special stress on individual discovery, on first-hand experience and on opportunities for creative work…Older virtues, as they are usually called, of neatness, accuracy, care and perseverance are genuine virtues and an education which does not foster them is faulty.

The impact on pupils

At some schools, especially in the Inner London Education Authority (ILEA), some liberal teachers and headteachers took such reforms to an extreme: they introduced relaxed discipline, teachers were called by their first name and there was no school uniform. In at least one school (William Tyndale Junior School) pupils could watch TV or play table tennis if they did not feel like studying! Many parents became concerned about 'trendy teachers' and about the lack of discipline and learning in many schools, as teachers in some secondary schools also introduced reforms from the Plowden Report. Some genuine fears were made worse by a stream of sensationalist stories in the press and by the harsh depiction of comprehensive schools in the hit TV series *Grange Hill* (first screened in 1978).

Source B	A photo from the 1967 Plowden Report.

Activities

1. Compare Source B with Source B on page 11. How would you summarise the key differences? How would you explain the reasons for the differences?

2. Summarise Source A in your own words. Aim to use as few words as possible.

Pupils' educational opportunities were affected more by other educational reforms than the change to comprehensive education itself.

- Only the top 20 per cent of students took O-Levels; the rest left with no qualifications until a new exam called the CSE was introduced in 1965. Pupils at comprehensives were streamed into CSE or O-Level classes. The numbers taking O-Levels remained at 20 per cent but many more students now left with some qualifications. While there was a greater range of subjects for CSE, they were quickly seen as a second-class qualification by employers.

- The 1972 Education (Work Experience) Act raised the compulsory school leaving age from 15 to 16. It also allowed LEAs to set up work experience in place of lessons for final-year students. This helped school leavers find work in the tough economic climate of the mid-1970s.

- More pupils went to university but this was a result of government funding to boost the number of places available at new universities such as Sussex and Kent. The removal of the need for 'O' Level Latin at some universities also increased applications from comprehensive schools where the subject was often not taught. Nine per cent of 18–19-year-olds went to university in 1970 compared with only 5 per cent in 1960.

Exam-style question

1 Study Source E. What do you think was the purpose of this cartoon? Use details from the source and your own knowledge to explain your answer. **(8 marks)**

2 Study Sources C and D. How reliable are Sources C and D as evidence of the impact of progressive education in the 1960s and 70s? Explain your answer using Sources C and E and your own knowledge. **(10 marks)**

Source C — *From a 1965 report on comprehensive schools in Leicestershire for the* Times Educational Supplement..

> The schools are vigorous and self-confident communities... Both headmasters and staff are convinced that the academic child gets as good an education as in the Grammar school.

Source D — *From a speech in Parliament by MP for Islington George Cunningham on 5 November 1975.*

> On 22 September, the head and most of the teachers went on strike because ILEA [Inner London Education Authority] decided to carry out an inspection and inquiry. A temporary team was installed in William Tyndale Junior School and is still there. Imagine the disruption that this means for the children. Whoever is at fault it is not the children, but it is they who are suffering very greatly. There can be strong criticism of telling the young teachers to stick to the old ways. But what we have done is run down that system and put nothing in its place except the idea that each teacher is his own master, and entitled to do his own thing.

Source E — *A cartoon in the* Daily Express *published on 17 April 1977.*

"Parents! Mind your own business! Give us your child at the age of six and he's ours for ever!"

29

Changes in British employment

> ## Learning objectives
>
> In this chapter you will learn about:
> - changes in the British economy that affected British workers
> - changes in employment law that affected women and industrial relations.

Economic change

Between the 1950s and 1990s, Britain gradually changed from an industrial to a 'post-industrial' economy: 'blue-collar' work (jobs in industry and manufacturing) declined while 'white-collar' work (jobs in offices or in the service sector) increased. The change was not an easy one and regions where most jobs were in older industries suffered in particular: Lancashire (textiles), Glasgow (ship-building) and Tyneside or South Wales (coal-mining) suffered far more than London (commerce). There were several reasons for the decline of blue-collar work:

- Britain was the first nation to industrialise. Other countries (such as Germany and Japan) caught up and overtook Britain. They used more modern technology that began to produce better products more cheaply.
- Britain had used its Empire as a large captive market for its manufactured products. The loss of the Empire (mostly between 1947 and 1963) meant more foreign competition for British manufacturers.
- Britain had large and powerful **trade unions** that worked hard to secure the best wages for their members; high wages increased the cost of British products and made them uncompetitive.
- British governments had made full employment their top priority in their economic policy (many could remember the terrible time of mass unemployment during the Great Depression in the 1930s). They preferred to preserve jobs rather than promote efficient production. This allowed older British industries to become uncompetitive by the 1970s, leading to redundancies amongst blue-collar workers.

| **Source A** | A table showing Britain's share of the global manufacturing trade. |

Year	1950	1960	1970
Share (%)	25	17	10

| **Source B** | A table showing the percentages of people in England and Wales employed in different types of job. |

Share (%)	1951	1961	1971	1981
Agriculture and Fishing	4.8	3.4	2.8	2.2
Energy and water	6.8	4.7	6.0	7.3
Construction	6.2	6.7	7.1	6.9
Manufacturing	36.3	36.3	31.7	23.1
Services	45.8	48.8	52.4	60.5

There were also several reasons for the growth of white-collar work:

- Higher disposable income fuelled an increased demand for goods and services, that had previously been seen as unaffordable luxuries; this created more jobs.
- Governments increased spending on services such as health and education; this created a lot more **public sector** jobs.
- It is far more difficult to mechanise white-collar jobs than manufacturing jobs; fewer white-collar than blue-collar jobs were lost through **automation**.

Many women benefitted from these changes: it was felt that white-collar jobs were far more suitable for women than those in industry. There was also far more part-time white-collar work available than there had been in blue-collar industries; this allowed women to balance a job with family life. Not all women were satisfied: they were still paid on average 59 per cent the hourly pay of a male worker.

Employment law – women in work

Successive governments passed some important Acts of Parliament in the 1970s that attempted to respond to the economic changes affecting the British economy. Three Acts aimed to outlaw discrimination in female employment:

- The Equal Pay Act (1970) called for 'equal pay for equal work'. It remained voluntary for businesses until 1975. Many employers (in 80 per cent of cases successfully) claimed that the work men and women did was different so the law did not apply. This loophole was removed in 1983 by replacing 'equal work' with 'work of comparable value'.

- The Sex Discrimination Act (1975) made it illegal to treat workers of one gender less favourably than those of the other gender. While this helped in theory, in practice it was difficult and expensive for women to bring their discrimination claims to court.

- The Employment Protection Act (1975) made it illegal to sack women because they were pregnant; it gave women the right to maternity pay and to return to their jobs if they wished.

Employment law – industrial relations

A further range of Acts aimed (but failed) to improve relations between employers and employees and reduce the number of strikes (see pages 32–37):

- The Industrial Relations Act (1971), the Trade Union and Industrial Relations Act (1974) and the Employment Protection Act (1975) all tried to achieve this.

- The Health and Safety at Work Act (1974) was the first of many similar acts that have successfully improved working conditions.

Exam-style question

Study Source C and use your own knowledge. What was the purpose of this photograph? Use details from the photograph and your own knowledge to explain your answer. (8 marks)

Activities

1 Discuss the following questions in pairs and then share your ideas with the class:

  a How might the changes in employment outlined above impact on people's lives?

  b How important are jobs to people's identities?

  c Are certain jobs associated with a particular class?

2 a Study Sources A and B. How useful are the statistics to an historian who wants to learn about the British economy and employment in the 1960s and 1970s?

  b What are the key advantages and disadvantages of statistical evidence?

Source C *Female bus company employees protesting over equal employment rights in 1965.*

When the lights went out: the three-day week

Learning objectives

In this chapter you will learn about:

● the failure of government efforts to fix the economy

● the causes of, and popular reactions to, the three-day weeks in 1972 and 1974.

State of Emergency

A State of Emergency is declared by the government in times of extreme risk to public security; it allows the government to enforce certain rules with temporary extra powers. Five States of Emergency were declared between 1970 and 1973! In February 1972, businesses were forced to use electricity on only three consecutive days per week, a so-called 'three-day week'; as production slowed, 800,000 workers were sent home. Electricity was not to be used for heating shops, offices or leisure venues. The BBC and ITV were told to stop broadcasting after 10.30pm. In November 1973 the government banned floodlighting and electric advertising; on New Year's Eve 1973 another 'three-day week' was declared; this one lasted for two months! Energy supplies were clearly the problem, but why? And why did the government fail to address the problem?

Source A *A photo of the mass picket at the Saltley coal depot, Birmingham on 9 February 1972.*

Who was to blame for the lights going out?

There were two potential culprits for the States of Emergency: the government and the trade unions, particularly the National Union of Miners (NUM). Each side blamed the other and historians have been divided on the issue. The changing industrial landscape (see pages 30–31) was at the root of the problem but the trigger was the competing goals and methods of the government and the NUM.

The government wanted to:

● keep unemployment and inflation (the rate of change in average prices) low

● keep spending on imports lower than profits made through exports

● maintain law and order.

It could use levels of government spending, taxation and interest rates to control economic growth. It could also try to control the wage-demands of trade unions, either with binding legislation (wage-caps) or through voluntary agreements with the unions.

The NUM wanted to:

● ensure that its members' wages kept up with (or ideally exceeded) inflation. They argued that mining is a dirty and dangerous job and should be well-paid.

The NUM, like other trade unions, could go on strike if negotiations with employers failed. Workers could limit the work they did (for example by imposing a ban on overtime) or could stop work altogether. Strikes could be official (legal and organised with advance warning by union leaders) or unofficial (illegal and organised by workers with no warning). They could form **picket lines** to stop anyone getting into the mine or factory.

Activity

Read the details of the negotiations between the miners and the two different governments below and then write a paragraph explaining who you think was most to blame for the emergencies: the government or the trade unions.

Labour Government: We own the mines but they are losing us too much money! We had to sack 420,000 miners in the 1960s to keep the industry afloat!

NUM: We understand but the miners are getting angry: they keep seeing other workers' wages going up at a higher rate and worry about who will be sacked next!

Labour Government Employment Secretary Barbara Castle: We want to help you but you must agree to the proposals in my document 'In Place of Strife':

● you must **ballot** for strike action if it causes serious problems

● workers on unofficial strike must return to work after a 28-day 'cooling off' period

● your disputes with other unions must be judged by a new Industrial Board.

NUM: Not a chance! Trade unions sponsor 150 Labour MPs and this is how you thank us!

Conservative government: You don't sponsor our MPs and now we're going to force you to accept changes with our 1971 Industrial Relations Act:

● Strike ballots are compulsory.

● No more **closed shop**: workers can get a job without joining a trade union.

● Unions must sign up to an Industrial Relations Court.

We're also going to cap wage increases at 8 per cent!

NUM: We want a 33 per cent wage increase. After 5 months of useless negotiations, all 280,000 miners are going on strike on 8 January 1972!

NUM activist Arthur Scargill: Let's use **flying pickets** to shut down coal distribution depots and power stations!

Conservative Government: How about 12 per cent?

NUM: No.

Conservative Government: STATE OF EMERGENCY! Final offer: 27 per cent?

NUM: No. Well, alright, as long as you throw in free work clothes and transport to the pit. We'll go back to work today, 19 February 1972.

The miners had won but the government was keen to control inflation to avoid another State of Emergency. Therefore in January 1973 it set up:

● the Pay Board to examine wage deals that affected more than 1000 workers

● the Price Commission to limit price increases for some companies.

Neither measure calmed things down. In February teachers, hospital staff, train drivers, Ford car workers and gasmen went on strike for higher wages. The government attempted further wage and price controls in October but, as you will see in the next chapter, the timing could not have been worse.

examzone
Build better answers

Use Source A and your own knowledge to explain why the lights went out in February 1972. **(10 marks)**

■ **A basic answer (level 1)** makes a simple statement from the source or from own knowledge (for example, *many people gathered to stop the coal being delivered*).

● **A good answer (level 2)** makes supported statements. Better answers in level 2 will use both the source **and** own knowledge to support statements (for example *Source A shows a picket blocking the entrance to the coal depot. This aimed to stop fuel getting to power stations and thus cut electricity supplies*).

▲ **A better answer (level 3)** answers at level 2, but explains the supported statements (for example ,… *The miners forced power cuts to secure their wage demand which they had failed to achieve with five months of talks*).

The 1973 oil crisis

> ## Learning objectives
>
> In this chapter you will learn about:
> - the causes of a weak economic situation by 1973
> - the 1973 oil crisis and its impact on Britain.

The 'dash for growth'

The British economy was in serious trouble by October 1973. The Conservative Prime Minister Edward Heath and the Chancellor of the Exchequer Anthony Barber both believed that the best way to solve both unemployment and inflation was to promote rapid economic growth. Tax cuts, increased government spending and lower interest rates in the 1971 and 1972 **budgets** led to the 'Barber boom'.

Unfortunately, the 'dash for growth' was a gamble that did not pay off: long-term problems in industry meant the only results were higher inflation and even more spending on imports. The government had to slam the brakes on spending if Britain was to avoid going bankrupt. In December 1973 the government slashed public spending by £1.2 billion and increased interest rates to 13 per cent. Job losses began to increase as a result; many trade unions organised strikes to fight job cuts. The NUM ordered an overtime ban while it once again negotiated for higher wages. Britain was already facing a fuel shortage when the worst possible thing happened – 2,300 miles away.

War and the oil crisis

On 6 October 1973 Egyptian and Syrian forces launched what became known as the Yom Kippur War with a surprise attack on Israel. Three days later the Americans, key supporters of the Israelis, began to airlift supplies to Israel. The Arab nations could not fight America directly but they had one way to fight back: increasing the price and cutting supplies of oil. Oil is vital for industrial societies and the Arab members of the Organisation of Petroleum Exporting Countries (OPEC) supplied huge amounts of it to America. On 16 October they raised their oil prices by 70 per cent; by 1974 the price of oil had increased by 400 per cent!

For Britain this meant:

- In the short-term, the high cost of oil strengthened the miners' position as they produced the coal that was the only real alternative energy source to oil. The government had to impose another three-day week to avoid an energy crisis. The loss of production caused a lot of temporary unemployment.

- In the longer-term, high energy costs also led to higher inflation and more spending on imports. This wrecked government attempts to control prices and wages, and forced them to impose more cuts in spending. This caused a lot of tension in the later 1970s and contributed to the 'Winter of Discontent' 1978–9 (see pages 36–37).

Source A	*From a BBC interview with NUM President Joe Gormley on 13 December 1973.*

The supplies of cheap oil are finished forever. The government are going to need more coal to fill the gap. And they won't have anybody to do that because men in Britain will not continue to work at the coalfaces for less than £40 a week. If the country doesn't see the sense of our argument then woe betide them for the future.

Activities

1 Write a diary entry for 7 days based during the three-day week. Make sure you use plenty of evidence to help explain the causes of the three-day week and what effects it would have had.

Source B *Modern historian, Dominic Sandbrook, comments on the impact of the three-day week in January and February 1974, from his 2010 book* State of Emergency.

There were reports of people queuing outside shops for bread, candles, paraffin, toilet paper and cans of soup. Motorists besieged the pumps to fill their tanks…But contrary to widespread belief, the three-day regime did not see widespread power cuts. Although demand for candles went through the roof most people barely needed them. The weather was so mild that after less than three weeks, it was already clear that the predictions of blackouts and anarchy had been wildly exaggerated.

Did you know?

The Ugandan dictator, Idi Amin, launched a Save Britain Fund in December 1973 to help his country's former colonial masters!

examzone

Build better answers

How reliable are Sources A and C as evidence of the impact of the 1973 oil crisis? Explain your answer using Sources A and C and use your own knowledge. (10 marks)

■ **A basic answer (level 1)** unexplained comment on reliability (for example, *Source A is reliable because it is an interview from the time*).

● **A good answer (level 2)** an explained judgement on reliability based on the content **or** the nature/origin/purpose of the sources (for example *Source C is reliable because it shows the impact of heating cuts imposed by the government to limit the use of energy*).

▲ **A better answer (level 3)** as for level 2 but uses content **and** the nature/origin/purpose of **both** sources (for example *Source C might be staged to look more dramatic to sell more newspapers: there are candles on the table despite lights on in the background*).

Source C *Women in the office of a duvet-making factory try to keep warm while they work in January 1974.*

Strikes in the 1970s

Learning objectives

In this chapter you will learn about:

- the 1974 miners' strike
- the public sector strikes that led to a 'Winter of Discontent'.

Why did the miners go on strike in 1974?

High inflation caused by the 'dash for growth' and the oil crisis led to even higher wage demands. The government wanted to limit wage increases to 8 per cent but the NUM, remembering their successful strike in 1972, wanted a 35 per cent increase! Other trade unions, organised under the Trades Union Congress (TUC), promised not to increase their wage demands if the government treated the miners as a special case, but Chancellor Anthony Barber said no to the miners. On 4 February 1974, 81 per cent of miners voted to go on strike. Three days later Prime Minister Edward Heath called an early general election: to the voters he put the simple question 'Who governs Britain?'. Heath narrowly lost the election and a new, Labour government was formed.

Source A	From a TV broadcast by Prime Minister Edward Heath on 7 February 1974

The issue before you is a simple one. Do you want Parliament and the elected Government to fight strenuously against inflation? Or do you want them to abandon the struggle against rising prices under pressure from one particularly powerful group of workers? It's time for you to say to the extremists and militants: we've had enough.

Activities

1 Create a poster, either for Edward Heath's February 1974 election campaign or to promote support for the NUM strike.

2 Which side do you think was more to blame for the strike: the government or the NUM? Have a class discussion.

Did the miners win?

The new Labour government backed down from confrontation with the miners. After a month of NUM strikes the miners were awarded a 32 per cent wage increase. Instead of wage-caps, the government negotiated a 'Social Contract' with the TUC. This trusted the unions to regulate their own wage demands rather than force them to accept government-set pay increases. The miners had won this battle but would go on to lose the war in their clash with Margaret Thatcher's Conservative government during the 1980s.

Why was there a 'Winter of Discontent' in 1978–9?

The winter of 1978-9 was the coldest since the 1940s. With roads blocked by ice and snow, the UK became increasingly paralysed by the worst wave of strikes since 1926. In 1978, James Callaghan's Labour government was determined to keep inflation under control and called for a 5 per cent limit to pay increases. However, prices were still rising at a rate that worried many workers; they wanted to make sure their wages kept up with prices and fairly reflected the value of their work:

- In September 1978, workers at several Ford car factories went on strike; by November they had won a 17 per cent pay rise. This smashed the government's proposed limit.
- On 3 January 1979, oil-tanker and lorry drivers went on strike. The tanker drivers quickly won a pay rise and returned to work. The lorry drivers held out for 6 weeks. In that time they not only refused to deliver goods but also picketed ports to stop supplies reaching industry, shops and even hospitals. People began to panic buy in case the shops ran out of food.
- On 22 January, 1.5 million public-sector workers went on strike: almost all schools shut, as did museums, libraries and other public buildings. With no porters, cooks or cleaners, hospitals were only able to treat emergency cases. With dustmen on strike, huge piles of rubbish began to build up in parts of towns and cities across the UK. In Liverpool, the gravediggers went on strike; by the end of January there were 225 corpses stored in a factory awaiting burial.

The government accepted defeat on 14 February and allowed pay increases of 10–15 per cent. By mid-March all those who had been on strike were back at work. The public had been frightened and disgusted by the impact of the strikes; a vast majority now believed that the unions were too powerful and that something must be done to limit their power. The Conservative leader Margaret Thatcher promised to do just that; and it came as little surprise that she won the May 1979 general election.

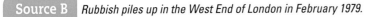

Source B *Rubbish piles up in the West End of London in February 1979.*

Source C *From an article by journalist Jill Tweedie, published in the* Guardian *on 18 January 1979.*

Wherever we turn, something has been cut off, due to an industrial dispute. Trains, planes, schools, petrol, newspapers, social services, hospital facilities and water, to name but a few. At the shops: toilet paper? Bread? Marge? Frozen peas? Sorry madam. All that went by 10 o'clock this morning.

Did you know?

Inflation hit a high of 27 per cent in 1975. Something that cost £4 in January would have cost over £5 by December!

Exam-style question

1 Use Source B and your own knowledge to explain why the winter of 1978–9 became known as the 'Winter of Discontent'. (10 marks)

2 How reliable are Sources B and C as evidence of the impact of the 'Winter of Discontent'? (10 marks)

38

In the Unit 3 examination, you will be required to answer five questions, applying your skills of source analysis to six sources on a topic from the Modern World Source Enquiry you have studied.

You only have one hour and 15 minutes to answer these questions, so the examiners are not expecting you to write huge amounts. The number of marks helps you judge how much to write. The time allocation below gives a little thinking time before you

put pen to paper and a few minutes to read through your answers at the end.

Question 1: 10 minutes

Question 2: 12 minutes

Question 3: 12 minutes

Question 4: 12 minutes

Question 5: 20 minutes

Here, we are going to look at Question 3.

examzone
Build better answers

Question 3

Tip: Question 3 will ask you to use a source and your own knowledge to explain why something happened. Let's look at an example.

| Source A | *From a BBC interview with NUM President Joe Gormley on 13 December 1973.* |

The supplies of cheap oil are finished forever. The government are going to need more coal to fill the gap. And they won't have anybody to do that because men in Britain will not continue to work at the coalfaces for less than £40 a week. If the country doesn't see the sense of our argument then woe betide them for the future.

Study Source A and use your own knowledge.

Use Source A and your own knowledge to explain why the 1973 oil crisis had a large impact on Britain. (10 marks)

Student answer

Source A says that one impact of the 1973 oil crisis was the end of cheap oil forever. OPEC raised the price and cut supplies of oil to punish the Americans for helping Israel fight the Arabs. This made oil more expensive for Britain.

Comment

This answer states that one impact of the oil crisis was an increase in the price of oil. It supports this statement by using the first sentence of Source A and own knowledge about why oil prices increased. Such an answer would be a high level 2. However, to be a more complete answer it needs to develop the explanation, not just support the statement.

Let's rewrite the answer to provide the detail.

examzone

Build better answers

Student answer

Source A suggests that one major impact was the end of 'supplies of cheap oil' and that more coal would be needed to fill the gap. By 1974 Britain had to pay 400 per cent more for oil imports than it had done before OPEC cut supplies to punish US support for Israel in the Yom Kippur War. Expensive oil contributed to high inflation and therefore to further wage demands and strikes. It also strengthened the position of the miners who took advantage of the crisis when they went on strike in January 1974. The oil crisis and the miners' strike forced the government to declare a three-day week. This was highly unpopular and was a major reason why Heath lost the February 1974 general election.

Comments

This is an excellent answer. It clearly explains how the oil crisis impacted upon Britain, firstly through higher prices and secondly by strengthening the miners' strike. It uses precise quotations from the source and detailed own knowledge to support the explanation. This would be a high level 3 answer.

Key Topic 3: Media, communications and leisure 1960-79

Mass media sometimes reflected society's opinions but also helped form them. The 1960s are often seen as a decade of great change, a period when traditional opinions were challenged, especially by 'teenagers'. However, were such changes in British society real and widespread or merely an illusion created by media hype?

In this Key Topic you will study:

- changes in the press, cinema, radio and record industry
- the growth of television and its impact on other leisure pursuits
- the 'Swinging Sixties': a revolution in fashion, culture and pop music or just media hype?
- youth culture and the rise of the teenager
- changes in leisure: sport, entertainment and holidays.

The TV times: mass media in the 1960s and 1970s

Learning objectives

In this chapter you will learn about:
- the rise of television
- the impact of TV on cinema, the press and the public.

Source A	From Mary Whitehouse's Manifesto for her Clean Up TV campaign, written in 1964.

We women of Britain believe in a Christian way of life. We object to the propaganda of disbelief, doubt and dirt that the BBC projects into millions of homes through the television screen.

The rise of TV

The 1960s and 70s saw television emerge as the dominant mass medium in Britain. The number of TV licences sold increased from 344,000 in 1955 to 18 million in 1979. Aside from the huge growth in audiences there were a number of important changes in TV broadcasting:

- Until 1955 the BBC was the only television broadcaster in Britain. Its first Director General, Lord Reith, wanted to give the public 'not what it wanted but what the BBC thought it should have' to improve cultural and educational standards. ITV began to broadcast in 1955. Many experts feared a 'race to the bottom' with 'vulgar' shows used to attract audiences and advertising revenue (the BBC was and is still funded by the Licence Fee rather than advertising). The 1962 Pilkington Report criticised adverts, game shows, crime dramas and Westerns for damaging moral standards in Britain!

- The 1964 Television Act forced ITV to show more plays and current affairs programmes and led to the launch of BBC2 in April 1964. This was to promote more public-service broadcasting.

- Broadcasts in colour began in 1967. 70 per cent of all TV sets were colour by 1979; this further boosted the popularity of TV as a form of entertainment.

The impact of TV on the public

In the late 1970s, people on average watched 16 hours of TV per week in summer and 20 hours in winter; this was twice as much as people in Belgium, Italy or Sweden. It meant that people spent far more leisure time at home; people of all classes watched the same shows and this blurred some class distinctions. TV also helped to spread new fashions more quickly; it became less easy to tell someone's class based on dress alone. With only three channels to choose from, some programmes gained huge audiences: 20 million regularly tuned in to watch Coronation Street (launched in December 1960) while 12 million watched the satirical show That Was The Week That Was (known by the shortened name TW3). This was the first popular show to make fun of politicians, including the Prime Minister, and even the Queen. Large audiences clearly meant such shows had the potential to influence popular attitudes. A pressure group, led by housewife Mary Whitehouse, was concerned about this influence and in 1964 started a petition to 'Clean Up TV'. She gained 500,000 signatures before sending the petition to the Queen. Although she became a household name, none of her criticisms led to any change. In 1965 she helped launch the National Viewers' and Listeners' Association (NVLA) which still campaigns against 'corrupting' TV under its new name Mediawatch-UK.

Activities

1 Imagine you are at the launch of the Clean Up TV petition. Half the class should prepare arguments for signing the petition and half against, before holding a class debate.

2 Split into groups. Each group should choose one of the following popular programmes from the 1960s and 70s to research:

   The Likely Lads, Steptoe and Son, Rising Damp, Are You Being Served?, The Good Life, Till Death Do Us Part.

   Use your research to find out about the main characters, typical plot lines and ways in which the programme might have affected attitudes.

The impact of TV on the press

The total sales of newspapers fell from 17 million in 1951 to 14.6 million in 1970. One reason for this fall in sales was that television news programmes were able to keep people up to date with current affairs, so they no longer needed to buy newspapers. To try to counter this, boost sales, and to win back some of the advertising revenue that had gone to ITV since 1955, newspapers became punchier and more sensationalist. Headlines grew larger and became more biting, large images replaced a lot of the text on the front page (Source C) and colour supplements were launched in 1962. The newspaper which took these changes even further was The *Sun*: re-launched by Rupert Murdoch in 1969, a relentless focus on television stars, sex, scandal and humour saw it overtake the *Daily Mirror* as the UK's most popular newspaper by 1979.

Source B *The front page of the* Daily Express *in 1960.*

Source C *The front page of the* Sun *in 1978.*

Activities

1 Look at Sources B and C. What similarities and differences can you see between the two front pages? How would you explain the changes in style?

2 It is 1960 and you are the editor of the *Daily Express*. Write a letter to the owner of the paper explaining why your sales are collapsing and what you intend to do to boost sales!

The impact of TV on cinema

The rapid rise of television caused cinema to also undergo change in the 1960s and 70s. The readily available entertainment programmes provided by television caused cinema-going to plummet in popularity. This had started to have some affect from the mid-1950s onwards with the introduction of the more populist ITV stations.

Newsreels suffered as they simply could not compete with television news coverage. Pathé stopped newsreel production in 1970 and British Movietone News in 1979.

By the mid-1960s many large cinemas were struggling to source enough films to show new ones each week, and this lack of variety caused even further closures.

British cinema seemed stuck in a vicious circle and of the 3,000 cinemas open for business in 1960, just 1,960 were still trading by the end of 1965.

Annual cinema ticket sales continued to fall from 340 million in 1964 to 140 million in 1974 (and a record low of 53 million in 1984). The loss of audiences meant a loss of American funding for the British film industry: 84 films were made in 1970, but only 41 in 1979. Many cinemas became run-down or closed and turned into pubs, nightclubs or bingo halls.

Source D	A modern historian summarises the decline of British cinema in the 1970s.

Most films were simply atrocious. Horror was the biggest adult genre of the day. Yet with producers hoping to win back audiences with nudity, sex and sensationalism, most horror films were incoherent affairs. The second biggest genre was sex comedies; unfortunately, not only were they not sexy, they were not even very funny. It is hardly surprising that most people stayed away. It seemed a reasonable assumption that cinema-going would die out entirely in Britain.

Exam-style question

Use Source D and your own knowledge to explain why cinema-going plummeted in the 1960s and 1970s.

(10 marks)

examzone
Build better answers

Study Source A and use your own knowledge. What was the purpose of this representation? Use details of the manifesto and your own knowledge to explain your answer.

(8 marks)

■ **A basic answer (level 1)** makes simple statements without using support from the source or own knowledge (for example, *It suggests the BBC was a bad influence*).

● **A good answer (level 2)** understands the purpose of the source and links this to details from the source and/or own knowledge (for example, *It was written to spread the message that the BBC undermined moral standards. It says the BBC projects 'dirt'*).

▲ **An excellent answer (level 3)** explains the purpose of the source using the historical context (for example, *It was written to persuade people to protest against what Mrs Whitehouse saw as immoral TV shows. The phrase 'disbelief, doubt and dirt' powerfully captures her concerns about new popular programmes such as TW3 and Steptoe and Son. People like Mrs Whitehouse were worried about the BBC broadcasting such 'vulgar' shows to compete for audiences with ITV after 1955*).

Rock 'n' Roll Radio

Learning objectives

In this chapter you will learn about:

● the significance of changes in radio

● the significance of changes in the record industry.

Radio

Radio did not suffer from the rise of television in the way cinema and the press did; this is largely because many people enjoy listening to music while they do other things. Radio became more popular in the 1960s and 1970s due to:

● the rise of portable transistor radios in the 1960s

● important changes to BBC radio broadcasting in 1967

● the sale of car radios in the 1970s

● the abolition of radio licences in 1971

● the growth of local commercial radio after 1973.

The BBC was the only legal radio broadcaster until 1973. It had been reluctant to play rock and roll music on the radio in the 1950s and 60s because of fears that it promoted rowdy and violent behaviour. The BBC limited rock and roll to one show, *Pick of the Pops*. As a result it began to lose younger audiences to new 'pirate' radio stations that transmitted from international waters to escape UK law. From 1964, Radio London and Radio Caroline were two of many pirate radio stations that specialised in pop music with fun, informal DJs. By the time the government tried to ban such stations in 1967, they had between 10 and 15 million listeners! The BBC was forced to respond: in 1967 it replaced the 'Light Programme' with Radio 2 and Radio 1, its first station devoted to pop music and younger listeners.

Source A | *From the* Sun *published on 28 July 1967.*

Radio 1, which starts broadcasting on September 30, will be very much like "pirate" radio, but without the advertisements. It will be promoted with happy-type jingles like "Radio One-derful" and big publicity campaigns for the disc jockeys. The head of the new station said yesterday 'Radio 1 would have no room for slouchers or fuddy-duddies. We will include DJs with a regional accent if he is good at the job'. After announcing their new look the BBC reported that "pirate" station Radio London will close on 15 August when laws to ban pirates takes effect.

Source B | *From the launch of Radio 1 at 7am on 30 September 1967.*

BBC announcer with 'posh' accent: It is my pleasure and privilege to launch Radio 1 and 2. We have done so to provide you with a better service of popular music and with more choice. It represents a new concept for BBC Radio: Radio 1 is designed to be young at heart and in style.

Catchy jingle: The Voice of Radio 1! Just for fun! Music! Too much!

DJ Tony Blackburn: Good morning everyone and welcome to the exciting new sound of Radio 1! So let's away!

Source C | *A teenage girl listening to a portable transistor radio in the early 1960s.*

The record industry

The UK record industry was dominated by two huge companies: Decca and EMI. Between them they launched the British stars of rock and roll, from Cliff Richard to the Rolling Stones and the Beatles. Their success was largely due to three inventions that helped the youth pop industry to take off:

- transistor radios – these were much smaller and more portable than older radios; they allowed young people to listen to pop music wherever they went.
- extended-play (EP) **vinyl** records – these were smaller and cheaper than long-play records (LPs) and only kept the most popular 4 to 6 songs from a whole album.
- the jukebox – these could hold over 500 EP discs; by 1960 there were over 7,000 EP jukeboxes in milk bars, coffee bars and cafes in Britain.

A combination of marketing by these huge companies, increased airplay of hit songs on transistor radios and the affordable nature of singles and EPs fuelled the rapid growth of the youth pop industry. Record companies further boosted the popularity of a few bands by allowing them to star in films: The Beatles' most famous films were A *Hard Day's Night* (1964) and *Help!* (1965).

Activity

1 Some have argued that transistor radios were as important to young people in the 1960s as mobile phones are to young people today. Discuss why you think this comparison has been made and whether you think it is a fair one.

2 If possible, interview older relatives or friends of the family about their memories of pop music and radio in the 1960s and 1970s. Share your findings with the class, either by recording the interview or writing out the questions and answers if this is not possible.

Exam-style question

1 How reliable are Sources A and B as evidence of changes in British radio in the 1960s and 1970s? (10 marks)

2 Use Source D and your own knowledge to explain how the UK record industry went from strength to strength in the 1960s. (10 marks)

Source D A poster for the 1965 Gerry and The Pacemakers film, Ferry Cross the Mersey. *Like the Beatles, Gerry and the Pacemakers were a popular band from Liverpool.*

THE BIG BEAT IS BACK WITH THE EXCITINGEST NEW PACEMAKING PACK!

Brian Epstein ___ **Gerry** AND THE **Pacemakers**

14 Fabtastic song hits!

"Ferry Cross The Mersey"

Cilla Black ___ Julie Samuel ___ The Fourmost
Michael Holden ___ Jeremy Summers ___ UNITED ARTISTS

The rise of the teenager: youth culture

> **Learning objectives**
>
> In this chapter you will learn about:
> - the rise of a separate 'teenage' identity
> - the nature of youth culture.

The invention of youth?

The word 'teenage' was not used until 1921; it was not commonly used in Britain until the late 1940s. Although older people have always been concerned about the behaviour of the young, there were several reasons why teenagers developed a more distinct, visible identity in the 1950s and 1960s:

- The post-war 'baby boom' meant there were over a million more teenagers in 1965 than 1951.
- A better, richer diet meant children went through puberty at a younger age (on average nearer 13 than 16).
- The extension of the school-leaving age meant starting work later: 15 and 16-year-olds spent more time with their peers than, for example, as apprentices in an adult workplace.
- The growth of production-line technology and service jobs meant unskilled teenagers could earn higher wages than their parents had done. With no rent or bills to pay, they had lots of money to spend on entertainment and fashion.

Source A *A modern historian on the nature of youth culture and how young people spent their disposable income.*

British teenagers in 1959 spent 20 per cent on clothes and shoes and just under 50 per cent on entertainment, from cinemas and dance halls to magazines and records. Young people accounted for more than 40 per cent of the markets for records and record players. Teenagers looked for products that were 'highly charged emotionally' and that offered something different from what their parents liked.

Youth culture

Youth culture was most clearly defined by music and fashion. Some of the most popular styles or identities in the 1960s and 1970s included Mods, Rockers, Beatniks, Hippies, Skinheads, Glam Rockers and Punks. For the vast majority of young people, such styles were purely about a sense of fun and identity. However, many adults, especially older generations, felt that British youth was out of control in a way that had never happened 'in their day'.

In truth, while there was a slight rise in youth crime in the 1950s and 1960s, and a sharp rise in arrests for possession of marijuana (up from 235 in 1960 to 11,000 by 1973), young people were no more violent, drunk or disrespectful than they had been in previous generations.

Source B *From an interview with Brian Harvey, a jazz musician in the 1950s.*

Barefoot dancing in the clubs, we were anti-establishment and anti-convention, though this, and our promiscuous behaviour was hyped up. Convention was still present, and I'd say from reading about the past that the Jazz Age of the 1920s was considerably more promiscuous than ours.

There were, however, some headline-grabbing clashes in the early 1960s between rival gangs of Mods and Rockers that fuelled this perception.

Activity

In your opinion, what gives today's teenagers a separate identity from children and adults? In groups, list as many ideas as possible and then have a class discussion about the most important reasons.

Source C   *Front page of the* Daily Mirror, *30 March 1964.*

Daily Mirror

3d. Monday, March 30, 1964 ◆ ◆ ◆ No. 18,746

Police chief sends SOS for reinforcements

'WILD ONES' INVADE SEASIDE—90 ARRESTS

By PAUL HUGHES

THE Wild Ones invaded a seaside town yesterday— 1,000 fighting, drinking, roaring, rampaging teenagers on scooters and motor-cycles. By last night, after a day of riots and battles with police, ninety of them had been arrested.

Groups of Mods and Rockers congregrated in numerous seaside resorts in south-east England, such as Clacton-on-Sea, Hastings, Margate and, most notably, Brighton in the early 1960s. There were often violent scuffles as the two opposing groups clashed.

These disturbances quickly caught the attention of the national media. The stories of youth, drugs, alcohol and violence were too good to pass up on and the media's relentless focus on this story reinforced the public perception of a rebellious and aggressive youth culture that was at odds with established authority.

The reality was that the violence, whilst concentrated, was sporadic and relatively small-scale, but the idea had been sown and the authorities responded. For example after the 1964 'Battle of Brighton', one Brighton campsite refused to take any teenage weekend campers at all.

Source D   *From* Weekenders *(1965) a confidential report by the National Association of Youth Clubs regarding the 'Battle of Brighton' clashes between Mods and Rockers in August 1964.*

There was a minority of youngsters who came looking for trouble. The observers report that Brighton is a Mod town. Rockers turned up throughout the August bank holiday, and this caused running fights. There were several ugly scenes, including hooliganism in the main shopping street. There is no doubt that this minority is coming, not to sleep rough for an adventure, nor to play about on the beach, but looking for excitement of a violent kind. This minority is a difficult problem, which needs to be tackled at source. The source is the neighbourhoods, council estates and metropolitan boroughs, from which the fighters come.

Did you know?

The AA and RAC would report large concentrations of motorcyclists or scooters that their patrols came across to the police to help highlight any potential troublemakers!

Activities

1   How far do Sources B and C suggest that teenagers were seen as a threat by adults?

2   Carry out some research on one or more youth culture groups. Find out more about their fashion, values and music and use your research to create a presentation to show the rest of your class.

Exam-style question

1   What can we learn from Source A about the nature of youth culture? (6 marks)

2   How reliable are Sources C and D as evidence of youth culture? Explain your answer using Sources C and D and your own knowledge. (10 marks)

Bigger than Jesus? The Beatles and media hype

> **Learning objectives**
>
> In this chapter you will learn about:
> - the causes and impact of 'Beatlemania'
> - the role of mass media in creating the 'Swinging Sixties'.

Beatlemania

If one band came to symbolise the 'Swinging Sixties' it was surely the Beatles, who had a rapid rise to fame and fortune in that decade. Formed as the Quarry Men in 1957, they were an obscure, struggling band until 1962 when they were signed by EMI. In 1963, following the huge success of singles like 'Twist and Shout' and 'Please Please Me', the *Daily Mirror* coined the phrase 'Beatlemania'. In 1964 they led the '**British invasion**' of the US pop charts; by 1965 they had released two movies and had sold so many records that they were awarded MBEs for services to British exports. In 1966, band member John Lennon humorously claimed the Beatles were 'more popular than Jesus'! While the quality of Lennon and Paul McCartney's catchy pop songs was the main reason for their success, Beatlemania would not have been possible in an era before the rise of pop radio, television and the teenager as consumer.

Source A *A photograph of the Beatles in 1963.*

It is surely no coincidence that the band really took off after taking on businessman Brian Epstein as their manager in late 1961 and being signed to EMI records by producer George Martin in 1962. This backing by one of the record industry giants led to huge publicity, airplay on pirate radio and sales of EPs and singles.

Bigger than Jesus? The Beatles and media hype

49

Did you know?

By 1970, Beatles merchandise (including hats, badges, shirts, socks, tea towels, mugs, ashtrays and hairspray) had sold for more than £100 million (£1.3 billion in today's money)!

Activities

1 The Beatles had scruffy hair and wore leather jackets before 1962. How would you explain their sudden change of image shown in Source A?

2 How far do Sources A, B, C and D support the view that Beatlemania was largely driven by media hype? Explain your answer using the content and the nature, origin and purpose of the sources.

Source B *A modern historian writing in 2005 about Beatlemania.*

According to the *Daily Mirror*, 'the police had to hold back 1000 squealing teenagers as the Beatles made their getaway'. A photographer recalled that they saw no more than eight girls, and a photograph printed in the *Daily Mail* showed one policeman and three girls. Three weeks later the crowds that awaited the Beatles [outside the Royal Variety Performance] were no figment of the imagination. When ITV broadcast a tape of the concert almost 26 million people tuned in to watch.

Source C *From the* Daily Mirror *published on 6 November 1963.*

YEAH! YEAH! YEAH! You have to be a real square not to love the nutty, noisy, happy, handsome Beatles. If they don't put a beat in your feet – sister, you're not living. Beatle people are everywhere. From Wapping to Windsor. Aged seven to seventy. Good luck Beatles!

Source D *From a magazine article 'The Menace of Beatlism', published in the* New Statesman *in 1965.*

Those who flock around the Beatles, whose vacant faces flicker over the TV screen, are the least fortunate of their generation, the huge faces bloated with cheap sweets and smeared with chain store make-up, the shoddy, stereotyped 'with-it' clothes: here is a generation enslaved by a commercial machine.

examzone — Build better answers

What can we learn from Source D about Beatlemania?
(6 marks)

■ **A basic answer (level 1)** just copies or paraphrases the source (for example, *Source D tells me that Beatles fans wore 'with-it' clothes*).

● **A good answer (level 2)** makes inferences (for example, *Source D suggests that Beatlemania was engineered by businessmen and mass media*).

▲ **A better answer (level 3)** answers at level 2, but then supports the inference (for example, *...because it says that their faces 'flicker over the TV screen' and their fans were 'enslaved by a commercial machine'*).

examzone — Top tip

'Paraphrase' means to repeat the same information with different words. You should avoid this and instead aim to make inferences. Inferences are judgements based on sources but not directly found in the source.

The invention of cool: the Swinging Sixties

Learning objectives

In this chapter you will learn about:

- the reasons why the Sixties have been remembered as a 'swinging' decade
- what people understood by the term 'swinging' in the 'Swinging Sixties'.

Swinging?

For people who did not live through the 1960s, the Austin Powers films sum up what most people imagine the 'Swinging Sixties' to have been like.

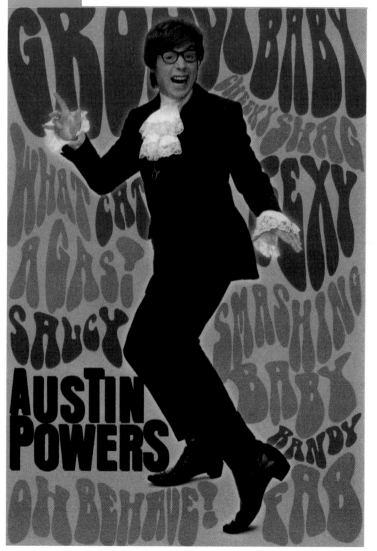

| Source A | *A poster for the 1997 film Austin Powers.* |

This modern perception is based on the mass media attention given to a remarkably small group of actors, models, designers, photographers and musicians who lived and partied in Central and West London.

Soho, and the fashion stores of Carnaby Street in particular, were the epicentre of 'Swinging London' from 1964 to 1967.

- Designers such as Mary Quant inspired new fashions such as Op Art and 'the Look' with the use of black and white (later bold colours) patterns and shapes.
- Biba was a shop which sold fashionable clothes at fairly affordable prices; there was only one shop in London but it sold mail-order throughout the UK.
- Celebrity photographer David Bailey and models like Jean Shrimpton and Twiggy, helped spread the popularity of new fashions in colour supplements. Mini-skirts became popular in the mid-1960s.
- The Mini became *the* fashionable car of the 1960s. It was affordable but was driven by many celebrities including all four Beatles.
- James Bond films such as *Thunderball* (1965) were globally popular and helped spread the image of 'Cool Britannia'. The Union Jack flag itself became a symbol of cool modernity.

Those who were part of 'the scene', or who wrote about it in the new colour supplements, defined 'swinging' as youthful, energetic, creative, sexy, high-spending and highly fashionable. They also described it as the cutting edge of a new 'classless' Britain that was sweeping away stuffiness and old social barriers: actors from working-class backgrounds like Michael Caine and Terence Stamp mixed in the trendy new discothèques with the sons and daughters of aristocracy.

For a while at least, London was the global trendsetting capital and American teenagers copied British fashions and slang. By the end of 1967, 'Swinging London' had become a tired cliché; America once again became a major influence on fashion with the arrival of the hippy movement.

Source B | *From a newspaper interview with the actor Terence Stamp in 1965.*

People like me, we're the moderns. We have no class and no prejudice. We're the new swinging Englishmen that I think the general public will be interested in. And it's people like me who are spreading the word.

Source C | *From Tom Salter's 1970 book* Carnaby Street. *Salter was the owner of the fashion store 'Gear'.*

In the early sixties only a few young men walked through on a Saturday morning, just to see what they ought to be wearing. Numbers grew, until from far outside London, youngsters would make this weekly trip, a kind of pilgrimage to the shrine of fashion. Now they come in coachloads, old and young, from all over Britain, and from all over the world after what is bright and new. All come to look, some come to shop, a few come to thieve. They photograph the street and themselves, even tape-record its sounds.

Source D | *A photograph of the Beatles in 1967.*

Activities

1 In pairs, look at Source A and make a list of all the inferences you can make about popular modern perceptions of the 1960s.

2 Still in pairs, see how many differences in style you can spot between the Beatles in Source A on page 48 and Source D below.

3 As a class, discuss how far such changes in style are a clear reflection of changes in popular values.

Exam-style question

How reliable are Sources B and C as evidence of the Swinging Sixties in London? Explain your answer using Sources B and C and your own knowledge. (10 marks)

Britain beyond Carnaby Street

52

The Swinging Sixties were about more than just fashion; the phrase also summarises a change in attitudes and values. Many felt that Britain was becoming more democratised: people from ordinary backgrounds could become famous and successful in creative industries, fashions obscured class boundaries and more regional accents were heard on TV and radio. A major symbol of this was the Mini, an affordable car that was driven by all four Beatles and even the Queen. Just as the Mini symbolised a supposedly new 'classless' Britain, so the mini-skirt and then the 'free love' of the hippy movement represented a more liberal attitude to a range of things, from sex before marriage to homosexuality.

Some politicians and historians have argued that the 1960s were a major watershed between Victorian values and the rise of a more modern '**permissive** society'. Others have argued that there was no real revolution in attitudes outside 'Swinging London' and that we should really refer to the 'cautious sixties'. These ideas are explored in depth in Key Topic 4, but, with regard to fashions and lifestyle, how far was the rest of Britain swept up by the 'Swinging Sixties'?

It takes money to enjoy a fashionable lifestyle, and poverty was a problem for many people in the 1960s. The 1966 TV play *Cathy Come Home* shocked many people with its portrayal of homeless life. The film helped to gain a lot of support for the new homeless charity, Shelter.

Source A — *Writing in 2007, Paul Nelson remembers growing up in 1960s Doncaster.*

The Swinging Sixties were a long time in arriving in Doncaster and as one of the few teenagers to have long hair from 1964 onwards, I endured many taunts and comments. However, the bravest thing I ever did was to wear a cloak on a date in 1967. The 60s was a splendid decade of awakening, but the scars of the time – inner ring roads and concrete slab constructions in place of fine old buildings – still remain.

Source B — *Writing in 2007, Lorna Westcott remembers growing up in 1960s Aberdeen.*

It was the decade I left school and started work. It was also the time when my friends and I bought and made our own fashions. For about the first time since the age of 13 we didn't all look like our mothers! For the first time, money in my pocket, films, music, books, magazines aimed at people like me. Oh those white plastic Mary Quant-style boots, the mini-skirt and those blue, mottled thighs! Well, I was in wet and windy Aberdeen at the time and I wouldn't want to change a minute of it.

Source C — *A modern historian writing about the Swinging Sixties in 2006.*

In truth, most people remained completely untouched by the swinging 'social revolution' that was supposed to be shattering the old boundaries and creating a new class. A poll published by the *Sunday Times* in 1966 suggested that the great majority of people were bored of hearing about 'mini-skirts, pop music and bingo', and wanted the media to spend more time on serious issues.

Activities

1 How reliable are Sources B and E as evidence of the impact of the 'Swinging Sixties' beyond London? Refer to the content and the nature, origin and purpose of both sources in your answer.

examzone
Top tip

'Evaluate' means to weigh up how far a source should be used as evidence when reaching a judgement. Think about the nature, origin and purpose of the source when you evaluate it.

Source D   *A cartoon from the* Sunday Telegraph *published in May 1966.*

THE **2** CULTURES
VISITOR'S GUIDE TO SWINGING BRITAIN.

Tourists once called London 'Quaint!'—
Now it ain't.
But you could call it, if you want,
Very Quant.

There they are, slim and sleek,
Coming from the new boutique.
There they go, sleek and slim:
Which is her and which is him?

England! That's the place to be
If you're fond of PVC,
And longish hair, The Rolling Stones,
Cups of tea and buttered scones!

Source E   *Two young girls in their home in November 1968. Their mother had been on the housing list to receive better social housing for nine years.*

examzone
Build better answers

Source C suggests that the 'Swinging Sixties' had little impact on Britain beyond London. How far do you agree with this interpretation? Use your own knowledge, Sources A, C and D and any other sources you find helpful to explain your answer.

(16 marks)

■ A basic answer (level 1) comments without any support or paraphrases sources (for example, *The Swinging Sixties scene had some influence on Doncaster which is outside London*).

● A good answer (level 2) makes a judgement supported by the sources and/or own knowledge (for example, *When Source D says you can't tell 'which is her and which is him' it suggests that the extreme fashions of London were a source of humour rather than something to be copied elsewhere*).

▲ A better answer (level 3) answers at level 2, but evaluates the evidence (for example, …*However, the cartoonist wanted to entertain conservative readers who were not the target audience of the Swinging Sixties scene*).

The sporting life: changes in leisure and entertainment

Learning objectives

In this chapter you will learn about:

- changes in the nature of popular entertainment
- the extent of change in popular leisure pursuits.

That's entertainment!

The most important change in popular leisure in the 1960s and 1970s was its domestication: the rise of television meant people spent a lot more leisure time at home than in public places. In 1970, 29 million people enjoyed gardening, making it the most popular pastime after watching television. There was a large rise in a range of domestic hobbies and far more people took an interest in DIY and home decoration. Shopping also came to be seen as a leisure activity rather than a chore, with the rise of car-ownership and out-of-town superstores.

Source A — *From writer and journalist Anthony Sampson's 1971 book* New Anatomy of Britain.

Britain is the greatest nation in Europe for handymen and potterers-about. The British live a withdrawn life, mowing lawns and painting walls, pampering pets, listening to music, knitting and watching television.

Source B — *From a survey of leisure activities in 1970*

Activity	Percentage of population who listed this as a pastime
Watching TV	97
Gardening	64
Playing with children	62
Going for a drive	58
Listening to music	57
Home decoration or repairs	53
Going to the pub	52
Cleaning the car	48
Going for a walk	47
Going for a meal	32

Source C — *The Chelsea FC captain from 1970, Ron Harris, gardening as his wife watches.*

A question of sport

Without doubt *the* major sporting event of the period was the 1966 World Cup Finals: not only were they held in England, but the host nation won the cup! Since the 1930s football had gradually replaced cricket as the national game and 32 million people saw the match on TV. In the late 1960s and into the 1970s the reputation of the game plummeted due to the rise of serious football hooliganism. The increase in violence was largely due to the increased numbers of fans who could afford to go to away matches and the tendency for older, married men to stay home: where young fans had once been restrained by older relatives or work colleagues there was increasingly nothing to stop them getting out of control. Things got so bad that many clubs built steel cage fences to keep fans off the pitch; British Rail cancelled their 'Soccer Specials' that had allowed fans cheap travel to away games after several train carriages were totally destroyed.

Sport was also an important part of identity for many people. In Wales, the rugby union team were a source of huge national pride, winning 8 out of 10 Five Nations tournaments between 1969 and 1979. Similarly for the Scottish, the defeat of England at Wembley in 1977 and qualification for the 1978 World Cup where England failed were major events.

Participation in sport was encouraged with the construction of sport centres. In 1970, there were only 27 in England; this had increased to 167 by 1974 and to over 500 by 1979. Access to swimming pools and health and fitness equipment was particularly important for female participation in sport: girls and women tended to be excluded from team sports like football (one girl went to the High Court in 1978 to successfully overturn her ban from playing for Muskham United Under-11s) and most did not enjoy popular male recreations like fishing or bowls.

Source D *Scottish football fans invade the pitch after a 2-1 win over England at Wembley in 1977.*

Activities

1 How far are sports and leisure activities important to British people today? Are they an important part of identity? Have a class discussion.

2 Create a table with columns for Source, Evidence, Reliability. For each source in this section, list what you can learn from the source and how reliable it is for finding out about popular leisure pursuits in the 1960s and 1970s.

3 Carry out some research about clubs or associations in your local area. How popular were they in the 1960s and 1970s? Have there been big changes in membership? If this is not possible, interview a relative or family friend about their memories of sport and leisure in the 1960s and 1970s.

Exam-style question

Use Source D and your own knowledge to explain why football often made the headlines in the 1960s and 1970s.   (10 marks)

Seasons in the sun: holidays in the 1960s and 1970s

Learning objectives

In this chapter you will learn about:

- changes in the holiday industry
- the impact on British culture of holidays abroad.

We're all going on a summer holiday!

The amount of leisure time for the average worker steadily increased in the 1960s and 1970s. From 2 weeks' paid holiday in 1960, this had increased to 3 weeks' in 1975 and 4 weeks' in 1979 for full-time manual workers. With more disposable income more people could afford caravans. By the end of the 1970s almost half the UK population had been on a caravan holiday. The caravan opened up parts of Britain like Devon, Cornwall and Glamorganshire, which had previously been restricted to the wealthy few with second homes. Ordinary people increasingly took advantage of longer holidays to go abroad. Resorts like Benidorm and Torremolinos in Spain became the most popular foreign destinations; British people were nervous of foreign travel and such resorts offered the familiar foods and comforts of home with far better weather.

As a result of caravanning and foreign holidays, the traditional seaside holiday declined in popularity and holiday camps began to suffer by the mid-1960s. This trend was accelerated in the 1970s when limits to the amount of money you could take abroad were increased in 1970. From 4 million foreign holidays in 1970, the number taken increased to 9 million in 1973 and 13 million by 1981. Package holidays represented only 1 in 12 of all British holidays in 1971. The growth of jet plane services to Spain and Greece boosted sales of package holidays, but there was a major dip in the mid-1970s due to the tough economic situation.

Did you know?

In 1974, poor sales and the high price of oil led to the collapse of the Court Line travel group: 35,000 Britons were left stranded abroad and 100,000 more were owed £7 million between them.

Source A	*Chorus to the hit 1974 song Y Viva España. It spent 6 months in the charts and sold 1 million copies.*

Oh this year I'm off to Sunny Spain Y Viva España! I'm taking the Costa Brava 'plane Y Viva España! If you'd like to chat a matador, in some cool cabaña And meet señoritas by the score, España por favor!

Source B	*Speaking in 1999, a clerk from Burnley remembers her first foreign holiday in the 1970s.*

Stepping off the plane at Ibiza airport was incredible. The doors opened, the heat flooded in and the smell of pine mixed with cigar smoke…Unbelievable. Coming from a grey northern mill town, you can imagine when we saw all the lovely white painted houses we felt we were in another world.

Activities

1 In 1968, the owner of Pontin's holiday camps thought the camps were 'dying on their feet'. Write a report for him explaining why this was happening.

2 What point is the cartoonist trying to make about British holidays and holiday-makers in Source C?

Cultural imports

While the British still made fun of foreigners, they became far more European in the 1960s and 1970s. Food and drink that would have alarmed previous generations became a common sight in supermarkets, restaurants and ordinary dining tables:

- Wine consumption doubled in the 1960s and again in the 1970s (up from 2.3 bottles per person per year to 12.6 bottles). Favourite brands included *Blue Nun* and *Black Tower*.

- Continental lager was only 3 per cent of the British beer market in 1960; by 1970 almost all pubs offered lagers like Skol and Carling Black Label.

- Greek and Italian restaurants became popular with exotic ingredients such as garlic, aubergine and fresh pasta. Many people were fooled by a 1957 BBC April Fool's joke that spaghetti grew on trees.

- Britain joined the European Economic Community (EEC) in 1973. This was the forerunner of the European Union. In the 1975 **referendum**, 67 per cent voted yes to staying in the EEC.

Source D *A popular TV comedy sketch from* Monty Python's Flying Circus *in 1972. Watney's Red Barrel was a popular beer.*

I've been on package tours several times and I'm fed up with being carted around in buses surrounded by sweaty mindless oafs from Kettering and Coventry in their cloth caps and their cardigans and their transistor radios and their 'Sunday Mirrors', complaining about the tea, 'Oh they don't make it properly here do they not like at home'. And then some typists from Birmingham with diarrhoea and flabby white legs saying 'Food's very greasy but we have managed to find this marvellous little place where you can even get Watney's Red Barrel and cheese and onion crisps.'

Exam-style questions

1 What can we learn from Source B about British holidays in the 1970s? (6 marks)

2 Use Source C and your own knowledge to explain why the typical British holiday changed between 1960 and 1979. (10 marks)

3 How reliable are Sources A and D as evidence of British attitudes to foreign holidays in the 1970s? (10 marks)

Source C *A cartoon from the* Evening Standard *in August 1962.*

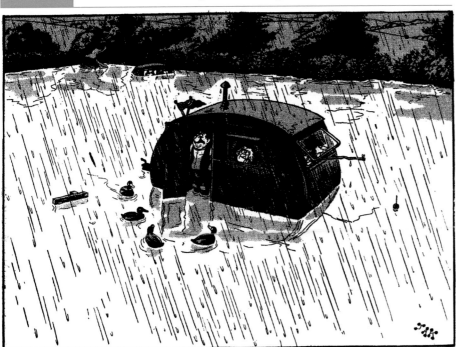

'Spain would be too hot, she said, couldn't stand Italy and all that spaghetti, she said, gambling day and night on the Riviera, she said, Greece was too far . . .'

58

In the Unit 3 examination, you will be required to answer five questions, applying your skills of source analysis to six sources on a topic from the Modern World Source Enquiry you have studied.

You only have one hour and 15 minutes to answer these questions, so the examiners are not expecting you to write huge amounts. The number of marks helps you judge how much to write. The time allocation below gives a little thinking time before you put pen to paper and a few minutes to read through your answers at the end.

Question 1: 10 minutes

Question 2: 12 minutes

Question 3: 12 minutes

Question 4: 12 minutes

Question 5: 20 minutes

Here, we are going to look at Question 4.

examzone
Build better answers

Question 4

Tip: Question 4 will ask you to judge the reliability of two sources. Remember that reliability means whether the source offers a full, accurate, trustworthy and believable version of the matter it relates to.

- On the one hand a source might have a trustworthy author but is unreliable because it only offers a partial or limited view of things.
- On the other hand a source might tell us lots of things but is unreliable because its author has an agenda, a reason to distort, embellish or lie!

Make sure you understand the things you need to weigh up when judging the reliability of a source before you continue. Let's use the sources on the Swinging Sixties on pages 52–3 (from Britain beyond Carnaby Street) to answer the sort of question you might get in the exam:

How reliable are Sources A and D as evidence of the impact of the Swinging Sixties in Britain? Explain your answer using Sources A and D and your own knowledge. (10 marks)

Student answer	Comment
I think Source A is reliable because he was there at the time, an eyewitness.	This answer offers a judgement but it is assumed rather than proven. It would only achieve level 1.

Student answer

Source A is reliable because it offers a balanced view of the Swinging Sixties. On the one hand he says how the fashions and ideas were 'slow to arrive in Doncaster' and how he was 'taunted' for his style. However, he also says how the 1960s were a time of 'awakening' and how he grew long hair and wore a cape! New fashions were an important part of the Swinging Sixties with the mini-skirt and 'beehive' haircut for women and the hippy style with long hair for men in the late 1960s.

Comments

This is a much better answer: it uses precise evidence from the sources and some own knowledge to support and justify an answer. This would secure level 2. However, it only discusses one source and so would be limited to 5 marks: you must consider both sources! It also fails to consider the nature, origin and purpose of the source to reach a judgement. This prevents access to level 3.

Let's rewrite the answer to provide the detail.

[continuing from previous answer]…A is also quite reliable because the author was an eyewitness to the impact of the Swinging Sixties. However, he wrote this almost forty years after the events he describes. There might be a touch of looking at things through rose-tinted glasses, especially when he describes the 'tremendous awakening'. Source D is also quite reliable as the cartoonist directly comments on some of the key aspects of the Swinging Sixties such as the fashions of designer Mary Quant and the music of the Rolling Stones. However, it was published to entertain readers of the conservative Sunday Telegraph and so exaggerates the silliness of the fashions, especially when it says 'but which is her and which is him?'.

This is an excellent answer: it not only does everything the previous answer did but also considers both sources. It also considers the nature, origin and purpose of the sources when reaching a judgement. A little more own knowledge on the music scene in the Swinging Sixties and a final conclusion on which is the more reliable source would have produced a more complete answer.

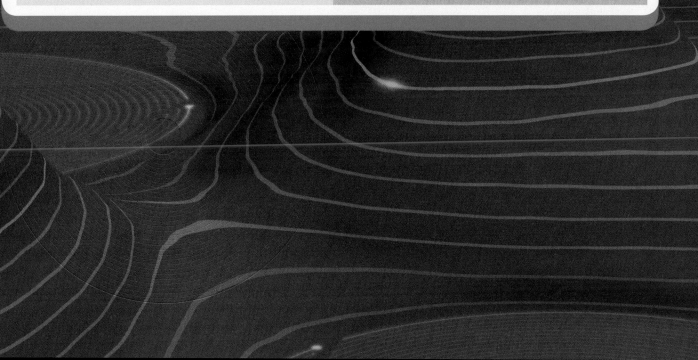

Key Topic 4: Reasons for social change 1960–79

From progressive teachers to permissive pop stars, some people increasingly rejected traditional values and attitudes in the 1960s and 1970s. However, although such people attracted a lot of media attention, this does not necessarily mean that most ordinary British people embraced such liberal outlooks and opinions. The key question is how far the attitudes of the majority of British people changed between 1960 and 1979 and the extent to which this change affected the lives of previously repressed, marginalised or disadvantaged groups.

In this Key Topic you will study:

- popular views on, and the causes of, the abolition of the death penalty
- the liberalisation of social attitudes to sex and family planning
- changes in racial legislation and popular attitudes towards minority groups
- the growth and extent of impact of feminism and Women's Lib.

The death penalty

Learning objectives

In this chapter you will learn about:
- the reasons for the abolition of the death penalty
- the impact of the Bentley, Evans and Ellis cases.

The abolition of the death penalty

The first major change in the law which can be seen as part of the 'liberalisation of society' was the abolition of the death penalty. On average, around 15 people were hanged each year in the early 1950s. Opposition to the use of capital punishment grew in parliament throughout the decade due to a number of controversial cases.

Derek Bentley

A policeman was shot during a robbery by two teenage boys in Croydon, south London in November 1952. The boy who fired the shot was only 16, too young to be hanged; his accomplice, 19-year-old Derek Bentley, was reported to have said 'Let him have it' before the shot was fired. Despite the ambiguous meaning of Bentley's words, his learning difficulties (he had a mental age of 11), and a petition for **clemency** by 200 MPs, he was hanged in January 1953. This led to a national debate in the media about the use of the death penalty. A campaign to clear Bentley's name was launched immediately after his death; this eventually led to an official government pardon in 1998.

Ruth Ellis

28-year-old Ruth Ellis shot and killed her lover in April 1955. Despite being the mother of a three-year-old child and the victim of abuse by her partner, Ruth was sentenced to death. There was widespread public and media opposition to the judge's decision; a petition of 50,000 signatures was rejected by the Conservative Home Secretary. The police had to be called to Holloway Prison the night before her hanging because a large crowd had gathered to protest. She was the last woman to be hanged in Britain.

Source A	A timeline showing Parliament's role in ending the death penalty in Britain.

1947 and 1956

The House of Lords twice blocked legislation to abolish the death penalty after the House of Commons had voted in favour of it.

1957

The 1957 Homicide Act limited the number of crimes that carried the death penalty to murder of a police or prison officer, murder caused by shooting or bombing, or murder while being arrested. It stopped 'joint culpability' for murder (which would have saved Bentley) and introduced 'diminished responsibility' (which would have saved Ellis).

1965

The penalty of death by hanging was replaced by life imprisonment for a trial period of five years (apart from for treason, arson in royal dockyards and violent piracy). This change in the law was made permanent in 1969.

Timothy Evans

Timothy Evans had been hanged in 1950 for the murder of his baby daughter. Evidence emerged in 1953 that suggested the crime had probably been committed by serial killer John Christie. After a long public campaign against this miscarriage of justice Evans received a posthumous pardon in October 1966. It was the first such pardon in British legal history.

The drive to abolition

Some level of opposition to the use of the death penalty had always been present in British society, but had mainly been focussed around pressure groups such as the National Council for the Abolition of Capital Punishment (NCACP). This organisation had been founded in the 1920s with a view to raising the profile of the abolition of the death penalty, particularly amongst MPs, and it enjoyed widespread support amongst public figures. By the 1960s, the group's membership included future Labour leader and Prime Minister, Harold Wilson, future Liberal party leader, Jeremy Thorpe and high-profile Conservative MP, Julian Critchley. The main figure of the NCACP from the 1940s onwards was Sydney Silverman, a backbench Labour MP.

Silverman was responsible for the first attempts to abolish the death penalty in the Houses of Parliament in 1947 (see Source A). MPs were given a free vote, meaning they did not have to vote on party lines, and Silverman's Bill was passed, despite the Labour government's opposition. However, the House of Lords blocked the proposed changes and the death penalty remained in effect.

One of the main arguments supporting the death penalty was the belief that it acted as a deterrent – the prospect of being hanged would put off potential criminals. However, despite a Royal Commission in 1953 on the issue reporting that there was no evidence that this was the case, support for abolition amongst MPs seemed to be falling.

Silverman continued to press for a law ending the death penalty and in 1956 another attempt was made. Once again, the law was blocked by the House of Lords. The Conservative government responded by passing the 1957 Homicide Act (see Source A). However, despite limiting the use of the death penalty it pleased neither side of the argument. The public also found strange anomalies in the Act difficult to understand; if you murdered someone with a stick you could not be hanged, but if you used a gun you could.

Activities

1 Have a class discussion about whether the death penalty should be re-introduced in Britain. In what ways might the Bentley, Ellis and Evans cases influence current thinking on the issue?

2 In groups of three, carry out more detailed research about public reaction to one of the following cases: Timothy Evans, Ruth Ellis, Derek Bentley. Use the research to produce a poster or pamphlet on why Britain no longer has the death penalty.

It soon became clear that the Act was not practical and by 1964, even the Conservative government realised that the death penalty would have to be abolished. Silverman had another chance in 1964. By that time, a more supportive Labour government was in power and Silverman's Bill was once again passed, with the support of 80 Conservative MPs. This time, the House of Lords did not block it and the death penalty was effectively abolished.

Source B	Notes of a Cabinet Meeting in December 1964, showing the support given to Silverman's Bill by the Labour Government.

It was agreed in discussion that, although there would be a free vote, any Ministers who supported the retention of the death penalty should preferably abstain from voting rather than vote against the Bill.

Exam-style question

1 Use Source E and your own knowledge to explain why the death penalty was abolished in 1969.
(10 marks)

2 How reliable are Sources C and D as evidence of British attitudes to the death penalty in the 1950s and 1960s?
(10 marks)

62

What about public opinion?

The death penalty had been abolished largely because a majority of MPs had been convinced by a long campaign by politicians such as Sydney Silverman. The majority of the British public remained in favour of capital punishment and support for it even grew in the mid-1960s. This was due to public horror at the crimes of the 'Moors Murderers', Ian Brady and Myra Hindley, and the shooting of three policemen in London in August 1966. While just over 60 per cent favoured the death penalty in 1945, this had risen to 67 per cent in 1965 and 70 per cent by 1970. The British public clearly saw death as the best justice for murder; they also felt that only the death penalty would deter people from committing murder.

Source C — *Historian Liz Homans writing for* History Today *magazine in 2008.*

The abolition of capital punishment did not reflect any sea change in public opinion, which remained firmly opposed to abolition. For abolitionists, the vote had nothing to do with any permissive society; it was the successful end of a long, long campaign.

Source D — *A headline and article published in the* Daily Express *in December 1965.*

MURDER WEEKEND.
The most violent holiday in London for years, ending as it began with a killing. There have been four murders in six days. That, for what the statistics are worth, is twice the average before the abolition of the death penalty.

Source E — Protestors demonstrating outside Wandsworth Prison, south London, in January 1953 against the execution of Derek Bentley.

Liberal Britain

> **Learning objectives**
>
> In this chapter you will learn about:
> ● liberal attitudes to sex and family planning
> ● the impact of liberal laws and the Pill
> ● the extent of change in attitudes to sex and family planning.

Liberal attitudes?

Traditional ideas about relationships between men and women included that there should be no sex before or outside of marriage, that marriage was 'til death us do part' and that abortion and homosexuality should remain illegal. The liberal ideal was far more permissive: homosexuality, legal abortion, sex before marriage and easier divorce should all be tolerated to promote greater happiness and well-being in society. Roy Jenkins, Labour Home Secretary (1965–7), proposed some important laws that were passed by parliament in the late 1960s.

Divorce

The 1969 Divorce Reform Act meant couples could end their marriage due to 'irreconcilable differences' after two years (or five years if only one party wanted it). Before this, one party had to prove that some fault or blame existed in the other in order to win a divorce through the courts. This was very difficult and expensive to achieve before the 1969 Act; some people were trapped in loveless or even abusive marriages.

The 1970 Matrimonial Proceedings and Property Act also made divorce easier as it recognised the value of women's work in the home. It also awarded women a greater share of a couple's wealth in the divorce settlement than was often awarded up to this time. Rates of divorce increased from less than 3 in 1000 marriages in 1965 to almost 10 in 1000 by 1976.

Source A — *From* The Labour Case, *a book by Roy Jenkins in 1959.*

Let us be on the side of people who want to be free to live their own lives, to make their own mistakes, and to decide, in an adult way and provided they do not infringe the rights of others, the code by which they wish to live; and on the side of fuller lives and greater freedom.

Source B — *A table of statistics on marriage, divorce and births, 1951–81.*

	1951	1961	1971	1981
Marriages per 1000 unmarried men	58	62	81	60
Divorces per 1000 married people	2.6	2.1	6.0	11.9
Percentage of UK births outside marriage	5.0	5.8	8.4	12.8

Activities

1 How far do you think people today have liberal views on homosexuality, divorce, pre-marital sex and abortion? Have a class discussion on whether liberal views are the best approach to these issues.

2 Which of the changes or reforms discussed above do you think would have the greatest impact on British people's lives? Explain your answer.

Family planning and contraception

In the 1960s and into the 1970s, the condom remained the most widely used form of contraception. However, the most important change during these years was the rise in use of the contraceptive pill. The Pill had been developed in America in the 1950s, but experts feared its introduction in Britain could promote **promiscuity** among unmarried women. This helps to explain the slow rise to importance of the Pill:

- The Family Planning Association had been set up in 1930 but only offered contraception and advice to married couples.
- Brook clinics offered the same service to unmarried girls as young as 16; the first was set up in 1964 but there was often opposition to the opening of new clinics.
- The contraceptive pill went on sale in 1961. Until 1970 only married women could get the Pill from their GP. This gave married women control of their own fertility. They could also pursue a career once their family was complete without the fear of an unwanted pregnancy.
- By 1969 only 15 per cent of married women used the Pill.
- It was not until 1974 that the Pill was freely available to all women through the NHS; this was liberating for some unmarried women.

Source C	*A poster from the Family Planning Association in the early 1970s*

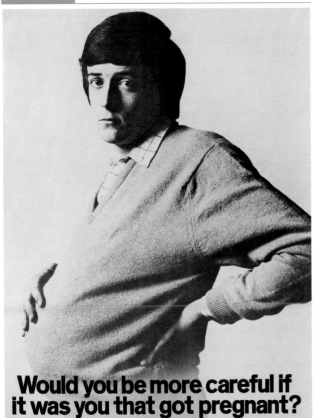

Would you be more careful if it was you that got pregnant?

Contraception is one of the facts of life.
Anyone, married or single, can get free advice on contraception from their doctor or family planning clinic.
You can find your local clinic under Family Planning in the telephone directory or Yellow Pages.

The Health Education Council
78 New Oxford Street, London WC1A 1AH.

Abortion

Abortion was only legalised in 1967. Before the Abortion Act, women who wished to terminate a pregnancy had to seek an illegal 'backstreet' abortion. These were often carried out by untrained people, usually in their own homes; the lack of hygiene and training led to 40 maternal deaths and over 100,000 injuries in 1966 alone. MP Dr David Steel used statistics like this when he persuaded Parliament to legalise abortion during the first 28 weeks of pregnancy. Opinion surveys carried out at the time showed that 70 per cent of the public approved of this reform.

Exam-style question

Use Source C and your own knowledge to explain how attitudes to family planning and contraception changed in the 1960s and 1970s.   (10 marks)

Homosexuality

Before 1967 (1980 in Scotland and 1982 in Northern Ireland), homosexual men ran the risk of arrest and imprisonment if they wished to have sexual relations; lesbian relationships had never been illegal in Britain. Many people thought of homosexuality as a psychological disorder that should be 'cured'. Over a thousand men were in prison in the mid-1950s purely because of their sexuality. There were several cases of blackmail of high-profile homosexuals and some were even driven to suicide.

The government-appointed Wolfenden Report (1957) recommended that private, consenting homosexual acts should be **decriminalised** for men aged 21 or above. However, there was a lot of resistance in parliament to such change, and it was not until the 1967 Sexual Offences Act that this advice was acted upon. For the vast majority of people in the 1950s and 1960s, homosexuality remained a taboo topic. Although there were some cultural signs that homosexuality was becoming more acceptable in the 1970s, it was not until the early 2000s that most British people felt it was not wrong to be gay.

| Source D | *Important events that helped the liberalisation of attitudes to homosexuality.* |

1971
First ever gay march in London.

1975
The Naked Civil Servant, a popular TV film about the homosexual writer Quentin Crisp, was screened by ITV.

1976
Tom Robinson released 'Glad to be Gay', which reached No 18 in the singles chart. Elton John and David Bowie admitted to being bi-sexual in the 1970s.

Activities

3 What can you infer from Source E about attitudes to homosexuality in the 1960s?

| Source E | *A poster for the 1961 film* Victim *in which Dirk Bogarde plays a homosexual lawyer who goes after a blackmailer of gay men. The film gained a lot of sympathy for homosexuals, especially among younger adults.* |

A SCORCHING DRAMA OF THE MOST UN-TALKED-ABOUT SUBJECT OF OUR TIME!

ALLIED FILM MAKERS PRESENT

DIRK BOGARDE   SYLVIA SYMS

VICTIM

ALSO STARRING **DENNIS PRICE** / A MICHAEL RELPH AND BASIL DEARDEN PRODUCTION / ORIGINAL SCREENPLAY BY JANET GREEN AND JOHN McCORMICK / PRODUCED BY MICHAEL RELPH / DIRECTED BY BASIL DEARDEN / RELEASED BY PATHÉ-AMERICA DISTRIBUTING CO., INC.

The elite vs the people?

While there were clearly some important legal changes in the late 1960s, it is less clear how far this changed people's attitudes. Some right-wing critics have claimed that the liberal laws were a 'victory for the elite over the people'. How far is this conclusion fair? While it is difficult to see into people's minds, three important surveys give historians an insight into popular attitudes to some highly personal issues:

● Michael Schofield's *The Sexual Behaviour of Young People* (1965) and *Sexual Behaviour of Young Adults* (1973). In 1965, Schofield randomly selected 1,837 teenagers from throughout the UK to answer a very personal survey. He used the same group for the 1973 survey.

● Geoffrey Gorer's *Sex and Marriage in England Today* (1971).

Activity

4 What are the advantages and disadvantages to a historian using surveys such as Gorer's and Schofield's to find out about sexual behaviour and attitudes to sexual issues?

| Source F | *From Schofield's* The Sexual Behaviour of Young People. |

The conclusion must be that sexual intercourse before marriage is quite common and acceptable among young people, although it does not appear to start as early as some people think or fear. When these young people seek sexual experience, in the majority of cases it is with someone they know well, and it is often with someone they love and will marry.

| Source G | *From Gorer's* Sex and Marriage in England Today. |

One quarter of males and two-thirds of females were virgins on their wedding day. 20 per cent of men and 25 per cent of women were married to the person they had first had intercourse with.

examzone — Build better answers

Study Sources B and F. How reliable are Sources B and F as evidence of British attitudes to sex in the 1960s and 1970s? Explain your answer using Sources B and F and your own knowledge.

(10 marks)

■ **A basic answer (level 1)** unexplained comment on reliability (for example, *Source B is reliable because it is a survey from the time*).

● **A good answer (level 2)** an explained judgement on reliability based on the content **or** the nature/origin/purpose of the sources (for example, *Source F is reliable because the results were based on a wide sample of randomly chosen British teenagers*).

▲ **A better answer (level 3)** as for level 2 but uses content and the nature/origin/purpose of the sources (for example ... *Source F also directly reveals that although sex before marriage was acceptable for teenagers, they were not generally promiscuous*).

Love thy neighbour? Race relations 1960-79

Learning objectives

In this chapter you will learn about:

● the reasons for and impact of the Race Relations Acts

● the state of race relations in Britain 1960–79.

Did you know?

Out of 2000 professional footballers in English teams in 1979, 50 were black; that year Viv Anderson became the first black England player.

Political and cultural racism

Contemporary media suggest that many British people still held racist views by the end of the 1970s. The media often showed racial minorities in a patronising or confrontational way, and compared with later decades there were far fewer sports or media figures who showed racial minorities in a positive, empowered fashion. There were a few films and shows that attempted to show minorities in a positive light, but they make highly uncomfortable viewing for audiences today:

● *To Sir With Love* (1967) A popular British film about an educated black man in London who accepts a job as teacher in a tough, mainly white, school. It was adapted from an autobiographical novel from 1959 by E.R. Braithwaite.

● *Til Death Us Do Part* (BBC 1965–75) A popular sit-com about Alf Garnett, a white, working-class man who expressed racist views which made him appear ridiculous. (However, many viewers shared the character's views and missed the point that he was being mocked.)

● *Love Thy Neighbour* (ITV 1972–77) A popular sit-com about a white couple trying to come to terms with their black neighbours. The white male was scripted to look ignorant compared to his more accepting wife. In contrast, the black male character is far more educated but also uses racism. The white and black women get on well together.

Despite this ease with the portrayal of racism in popular culture, there were only a few cases of public support for openly racist groups or politicians:

● In the 1959 general election, the founder of the British Union of **Fascists**, Oswald Mosley, campaigned against immigration; he gained only 8 per cent of the vote.

● In the 1964 general election, the Conservative candidate for Smethwick in Birmingham, Peter Griffiths, used the slogan 'If you want a nigger for a neighbour, vote Labour' as part of his successful campaign. Labour Prime Minister Harold Wilson said he should be seen as a 'parliamentary **leper**'.

● The National Front Party was formed in 1967. It firmly opposed immigration, as well as any measures to improve race relations and multiculturalism, with noisy demonstrations and marches. It had 20,000 members by the mid-1970s, but this support had collapsed by the end of the decade. It failed to gain a single parliamentary seat but caused widespread media reaction by gaining 16 per cent of the vote in the 1973 West Bromwich by-election.

Enoch Powell

In 1968, Conservative MP Enoch Powell made what became known as the 'Rivers of Blood' speech. He warned of a violent future for British multiracial society if the numbers of immigrants continued unchecked. Conservative leader, Edward Heath, sacked Powell from the Shadow Cabinet the next day; he never held a senior government position again. A petition to stop Powell being sacked gathered over 30,000 signatures. Opinion polls suggested that 75 per cent of the British public agreed with his speech.

Source A — *Enoch Powell, MP, speaking in 1968.*

A week ago I had a conversation with a constituent. He said: 'In this country in 15 or 20 years' time the black man will have the whip-hand over the white man'. I can already hear the chorus of complaints. How dare I stir up trouble and inflame feelings by repeating such a conversation? …We must be mad, literally mad, to permit the annual inflow of some 50,000 dependants. It is like watching a nation heaping up its own funeral pyre… As I look ahead, I am filled with foreboding: like the Roman, I seem to see 'the River Tiber foaming with much blood'.

Source B — *Smithfield meat porters march on the Home Office, bearing a petition that calls for an end to all immigration into Britain, 25th August 1972*

Source C — *A cartoon published in the* Daily Mail *the day after Powell was sacked from the Shadow Cabinet.*

Activities

1 Carefully study Sources A and C. How far do they suggest that Enoch Powell was a racist?

2 How far do Sources B and C suggest that the British public was racist in 1968?

3 In pairs or small groups, choose one of the following topics for further research: cultural racism (TV, film, newspapers, etc) or political racism (Oswald Mosley, National Front, support for Powell, etc.) in Britain in the 1960s and 1970s. Use your research to prepare for a class debate: 'This House believes cultural racism was a more serious problem than political racism in Britain in the 1960s and 1970s'.

Immigration and racial legislation

Source D — *Details of government attempts to improve race relations through laws to limit immigration and promote greater racial harmony.*

- The 1962 Commonwealth Immigrants Act meant immigrants from former British colonies had to have a prearranged job or skills needed for the economy to enter Britain. This was controlled through the issue of 'employment vouchers'. Many immigrants already in Britain now stayed permanently; they feared that if they left they would be unable to return. Such immigrants were more likely to be joined by their families. Despite this, opinion polls claimed that nearly three quarters of the British public supported the controls on immigration.

- The 1968 Commonwealth Immigrants Act meant immigrants needed, in addition to an employment voucher, a parent or grandparent who had been born in Britain in order to enter the country. This was criticised as a racist measure as it would allow far more immigration from Canada, Australia and New Zealand than from former colonies in South Asia, Africa or the Caribbean.

- The 1971 Immigration Act replaced employment vouchers with 12-month work permits so that immigrants could only remain in Britain for a limited period of time. By the early 1970s Britain had some of the toughest immigration laws in the world, virtually all black and Asian primary immigration had stopped.

- The 1965 and 1968 Race Relations Acts banned incitement to racial hatred and racial discrimination in public places. This made illegal the use of restrictions such as 'no coloureds' and 'Europeans only' used by some landlords and employers. The 1968 Act extended the ban on racial discrimination to housing and employment.

- The Race Relations Board was set up in 1966 to deal with complaints about racial discrimination. However, many saw it as a waste of time to use it: complaints could not be made about the police and only about 10 per cent of complaints to the Board were ever upheld.

- The 1976 Race Relations Act toughened laws against racial discrimination and victimisation. It also set up the Commission for Racial Equality to help fight injustice and create a fairer society.

Source E — *An extract from the Bernie Grant archives. Grant arrived in Britain aged 19 in 1963 and became one of only three black MPs in 1987.*

When I arrived here there were still the signs on the windows – no blacks, no Irish, no dogs, no children. Then there was the Race Relations Act of 1968, which outlawed all that. But what I found was that the problem lay in this **institutional racism**, hidden policies which you found in housing, in education and so on. There would be a policy which said that to get a house you needed such and such connections with the borough. Then they would define 'connections' as having your family living there for three generations or whatever. It was moving the goalposts, and it meant that black families hadn't a hope of getting a house. It was easy enough to deal with overt [clear and open] racism; you could fight the people concerned and that would be the end of it. The institutionalised variety just kept going. So I became involved with a lot of anti-racist work.

Multiracial Britain by 1979

Britain had become far more multiracial by 1979 than it had been in 1945. However, Britain in 1979 was still not a country where all citizens enjoyed equal political and legal rights, nor one where there was a positive acceptance of people from minority ethnic groups. Although curry had become a popular national dish and the Notting Hill Carnival had helped banish memories of the 1958 riots, this is not proof of widespread racial harmony. While racist language is now unacceptable, occasional racial violence and institutional racism in the police force since 1979 show how long and difficult a process it has been to build racial harmony.

Source F *The Notting Hill Carnival, 1971.*

Activities

1 Explain the difference between the 'overt' and 'institutional' racism mentioned in Source E.

2 How far do Sources D and E suggest that overt or institutional racism was in decline in the 1960s and 1970s?

3 Split into groups to carry out some more research on race relations in Britain. Each group should choose one of the following areas to research: film, TV, music, sport or political groups and individuals. Use your research to report back to the whole class. As a class, use all the research to decide how far race relations improved in Britain between 1960 and 1979.

CND and student protests

> ## Learning objectives
>
> In this chapter you will learn about:
> - the causes and impact of the Campaign for Nuclear Disarmament
> - the causes and impact of student protests.

CND

The Campaign for Nuclear Disarmament (CND) was founded in 1958. It aimed to promote public anger and civil disobedience against nuclear weapons, especially their presence in Britain. It organised marches, sit-downs and attracted some celebrity supporters such as the philosopher Bertrand Russell and actress Vanessa Redgrave (both of whom were arrested for demonstrating). The marches from the atomic weapons research site at Aldermaston in Berkshire to Trafalgar Square certainly helped to draw people's attention to the issue: 20,000 marched in 1959 and 100,000 in 1961!

Although 40 to 50 per cent of the marchers were under 21, CND support remained a minority interest for students. CND, however, failed to stop the British manufacture of nuclear weapons or the installation of American nuclear weapons in Britain.

Source A | *A modern historian's view of the impact of CND.*

CND never really seized the imagination of the majority because, although people did worry about the threat of nuclear annihilation, it frightened people in much the same way as the prospect of death; for most, it was something to think about while lying awake in the dead of night, but not something to have in mind when, say, buying a hat or eating a pie.

Activities

1. How far would you agree with Vanessa Redgrave in Source E that protests can achieve 'a heck of a lot'? Consider or research other protests such as the 2003 march against the Iraq War or the 2013 march against austerity and have a class discussion about their effectiveness.

Source B | *Police and protesters clash at Grosvenor Square, London on 17 March 1968.*

The growth of student activism

Increased government funding allowed the number of students to rapidly increase in the 1960s, up from 216,000 in 1962 to 310,000 in 1965 (see pages 26–29). Many became radicalised and politicised by opposition to the Vietnam War (1965–75). The American bombing of Vietnam was seen as an indefensible war-crime and thousands of students across Europe and the USA turned out for marches and rallies against it. The protests were at their most violent and radical in 1968 but quickly ran out of steam after this. This was partly due to divisions amongst the protest groups, but largely because most people did not particularly care about a war in which Britain was not taking part. Such protests also fuelled anger among some students against specific educational issues and against the capitalist system more generally. These protests turned violent on occasion but achieved almost nothing of note.

Source C Front page of Black Dwarf 27 October 1968. The newspaper had very few readers, mostly radical students.

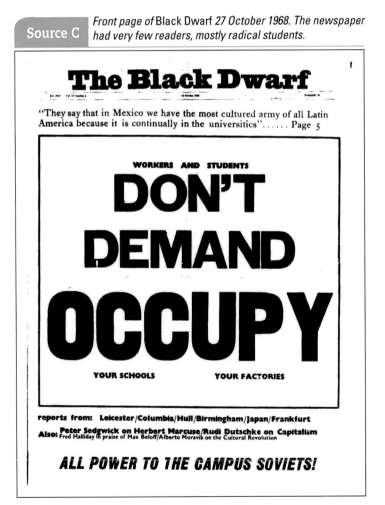

Source D An eyewitness description of a protest outside the American embassy in London, published in the Guardian in 2008.

On March 17 1968, there was a big anti-Vietnam war rally in Trafalgar Square in London. Afterwards, 8,000 mainly youthful protesters marched on Grosvenor Square, where a letter of protest was delivered to the American embassy. The crowd, though, refused to disperse, and a fierce battle ensued between demonstrators and riot police. Protesters hurled mud, stones, firecrackers and smoke bombs; mounted police responded with charges. The violence of the struggle, in the cosseted [pampered] heart of Mayfair, shocked everyone. By the end of the afternoon, more than 200 people had been arrested.

Source E Actress Vanessa Redgrave gives her eyewitness account of the anti-Vietnam protest on a BBC radio show in March 1968.

I don't think it was a very violent demonstration when you think of the history of demonstrations. There are always a very, very few people who are ignorant, not politically involved, and have come just for the excuse of a punch-up. The local paper reports give much more detail than the national newspapers: of the 5 coaches stopped on the way into London, reported in the national papers as 'bursting with weapons of marbles, red paint and pepper', in fact only 5 people on those coaches were charged with having those weapons. The march achieved a heck of a lot.

Activities

2   Look at Sources A–E. Rank them in order of which source offers the best evidence of student protests in the 1960s. Explain your order with reference to content and to the nature, origin and purpose of the sources.

Feminism and Women's Lib

Learning objectives

In this chapter you will learn about:
- the growth of feminism
- the impact of Women's Lib.

The growth of feminism and the Women's Liberation movement

Feminists argue for equality between men and women in all spheres of life, from wages and work opportunities to gender roles in the home and in the media. A second wave of feminism took off in the late 1960s (the first had secured the right to vote in 1918). This was partly due to the greater social freedom experienced by women during the Second World War, but was also due to some influential books and TV shows in the 1960s which portrayed assertive female role models. The points below highlight some key moments in the development of the Women's Lib movement:

- The National Housewives' Register began in 1960. Local branches organised meetings in members' homes, days out and an annual national conference. By the mid-1970s it had 20,000 members. This organisation reflected the boredom and frustration felt by many middle-class women in particular.

- In 1970 the first Women's National Liberation Conference was held in Oxford. The movement put together four key demands: equal pay for men and women, equal education and career opportunities for men and women, free contraception and abortion on demand, freely available 24-hour childcare. By the late 1970s, the Women's Liberation movement had groups in most British towns, cities and universities.

- In October 1970, Germaine Greer's book *The Female Eunuch* set out the feminist argument in forceful terms. It was widely discussed in the media.

Source A *Actress Dianna Rigg plays top spy Emma Peel in* The Avengers *(ITV 1961–9).*

Source B *The National Women's Liberation Movement march in London, 1971.*

- In 1972 the feminist magazine *Spare Rib* was launched; it gained 30,000 readers. The founders demonstrated against the 1970 and 1972 Miss World competitions.

- The Women's Aid Federation was set up in 1974. This organisation helped to develop facilities and support for women and their children who were suffering from domestic violence. This led to issues being discussed in Parliament and in 1976 the first Domestic Violence Act was passed. This made violence against both men and women in the home a criminal offence.

A feminist poster produced in 1975.

From an article in Black Dwarf *by Sheila Rowbotham published in 1969.*

We want to drive buses, play football, use beer mugs not glasses. We want men to take the pill. We do not want to be wrapped up in cellophane or sent off to make the tea. But these are only little things. Revolutions are about little things. Little things which happen to you all the time, every day, wherever you go, all your life.

Limits to the impact of Women's Lib?

Despite a lack of popular activism, feminists did help to shift expectations about what was acceptable at work and in the home for many women. However, this took time and in some areas of society there was little change in attitudes towards women and sexual discrimination by 1979:

- In 1970 the *Sun* newspaper used a topless model for the first time and by the mid-1970s the 'Page 3' feature had become a regular, yet controversial, feature of Britain's best-selling newspaper.
- Women's magazines, such as *Woman* or *Woman's Realm*, still focused primarily on traditional gender issues such as fashion, dieting, romance and the family. The most popular books for women in the 1960s and 1970s were fictional romances like those published by Mills and Boon.
- Only 10,000 women were active in the Women's Liberation Movement at its peak in the early 1970s.
- Children's toys in many ways reinforced gender stereotypes, as did children's reading books such as the *Janet and John* series and fiction such as *The Famous Five* stories. These were very common children's books and included stories and pictures such as boys helping dad clean and mend the car, while girls worked in the home with their mother.
- In schools, subjects such as Physics, Chemistry, Woodwork and Metalwork were still 'boys' subjects', while Cookery and Typing were 'girls' subjects'.

Activities

1   How far does Source A suggest that Women's Lib was promoted by mass media?

2   'The Women's Lib movement has been a success in Britain.' How far would you agree with this judgement? Prepare an answer and have a class debate.

3   Design a poster, leaflet or presentation that explains Women's Lib to a modern audience.

Exam-style question

1   What can we learn from Source D about the Women's Lib movement?   (6 marks)

2   Study Source C and use your own knowledge. What was the purpose of this representation?   (8 marks)

Women in work and politics

Learning objectives

In this chapter you will learn about:

- the impact of the 1968 Ford workers' strike
- the extent to which gender equality was achieved by 1979.

The fight for equal pay

Neither the 1970 Equal Pay Act nor the 1975 Sexual Discrimination Act might have been passed had it not been for a symbolic and successful women's protest in 1968. Female sewing machinists at Ford car plants in Halewood (Liverpool) and Dagenham (East London) went on strike to have their pay re-graded: their work making seat covers and headrests was classified as 'unskilled' and they earned less than male cleaners at the factory.

The strike successfully brought about the closure of both the Dagenham and Halewood factories for three weeks. They had the support of their trade union, much of the general public and the newspapers, although articles about 'plucky girls' and photographs of them having cups of tea seem patronising nowadays.

Finally, Barbara Castle, the Labour government's Employment Minister, was brought in to settle the dispute. The women eventually won a pay deal to put them at just over 90 per cent of the men's rate of pay for similarly skilled work. The women's strike at Dagenham and Halewood was a significant factor in bringing about the 1970 Equal Pay Act, although the Act was also passed to help Britain's application to join the European Economic Community (EEC), the forerunner of the European Union, where such legislation had already been passed.

Source A *Women from the Dagenham Ford car factory on strike for equal pay in London, 1968.*

Equal opportunities?

By the 1970s it was far more acceptable for women to return to work after having children. Women were also more likely to continue education past the compulsory school-leaving age and there was a significant increase in the proportion of female students at universities. Women were increasingly taking up careers in professions such as finance, medicine and law. But women were still disproportionately employed in lower-paid, lower-skilled jobs and part-time employment. Women were also under-represented in senior management positions and were promoted much less often than men. This has sometimes been referred to as the 'glass ceiling', an upper limit to women's promotion that is not made clearly visible but limits equality with men in the workplace.

Women in politics

Women remained badly under-represented in politics: out of 630 MPs in 1955, 24 were women; in February 1974 the figure was 23 out of 635 MPs. In 1975, Margaret Thatcher became the first female leader of a British political party; in 1979 she became Britain's first (and to date only) female prime minister. Her career exemplifies the extraordinary ability and determination that were required for a woman to succeed in a male-dominated environment. Thatcher herself did virtually nothing to help promote women into the higher offices of politics during her time in office.

Source B — British Prime Minister Edward Heath with 13 of the 15 newly elected Conservative women MPs outside the House of Commons in London on 30 June 1970. Margaret Thatcher is second on the right.

Source C — Margaret Thatcher interviewed in 1976 for the BBC Radio 4 programme Woman's Hour.

I didn't become an MP until after my children had started to go to school because I think that when they are very young they need mum. Mum certainly needs to be with them. Women who do their own job outside the home just have to keep going, in the evenings and at weekends.

Source D — From a speech by Margaret Thatcher on 3 July 1978 (the 50th anniversary of women aged 21 or over getting the vote).

Women are tired of being patronised and condescended to. We are bored by being considered as a curious and endangered species. If our homes and our families, remain central to us and our concerns, they are no longer our horizon.

Activities

1 How consistent are Margaret Thatcher's views on a woman's place in Sources C and D? How might you explain any differences in emphasis?

2 Look at Sources A and B. Which photograph do you consider best represents changes in the status of British women in the 1960s and 1970s? Explain your answer.

78

In the Unit 3 examination, you will be required to answer five questions, applying your skills of source analysis to six sources on a topic from the Modern World Source Enquiry you have studied.

You only have one hour and 15 minutes to answer these questions, so the examiners are not expecting you to write huge amounts. The number of marks helps you judge how much to write. The time allocation below gives a little thinking time before you put pen to paper and a few minutes to read through your answers at the end.

Question 1: 10 minutes

Question 2: 12 minutes

Question 3: 12 minutes

Question 4: 12 minutes

Question 5: 20 minutes

Here, we are going to look at Question 5.

examzone
Build better answers

Question 5

Tip: Question 5 will ask you to use a range of sources and your own knowledge to evaluate an interpretation. You will get an additional 3 marks for good spelling, punctuation and grammar. Let's use the sources on race relations on pages 69-70 to answer the sort of question you might get in the exam:

Study Sources A, C, and E and use your own knowledge.

Spelling, punctuation and grammar will be assessed in this question.

'Source E suggests that race relations did not improve in Britain in the 1960s and 1970s'. How far do you agree with this interpretation? Use your own knowledge, Sources A, C and E and any other sources you find helpful to explain your answer. (16 marks)

Student answer	Comment
Source A says British people were scared of immigrants taking over.	This answer shows some use of the sources but lacks clarity and development. It would only achieve level 1.

Student answer

Sources A, B, C and D all support the view that race relations remained poor in Britain in the 1960s and 1970s. Enoch Powell predicts 'much blood' if immigration continues to provoke racial tension in Britain. The cartoon suggests that Powell was correct in his speech and unfairly sacked from the Shadow Cabinet: the judges sentence him for 'speaking the truth'. 30,000 people signed a petition to try and stop Powell from being sacked. The Smithfield meat porters hold a banner saying 'Enoch is right' and the photo shows a large number of people marching in support of Powell. This support is supported by a poll which showed that 75 per cent of people agreed with Powell's views. The laws in Source D show that the government had to do something to ease racial tension. The weakness of the Race Relations Board suggests that the reforms did not have a large impact.

Comments

This is a much better answer: it uses precise evidence from the sources and relevant, detailed own knowledge to develop an answer. This would secure level 3. However, it is unbalanced as it only discusses evidence that supports the interpretation. Remember: you must clearly consider both sides of the argument to access Level 4.

Some evidence in Sources A and D suggests that race relations were gradually improving in the 1960s and 1970s. Enoch Powell realises his speech will be provocative when he mentions a 'chorus of complaints'. Racist groups such as the National Front Party were very unpopular: they failed to gain a single MP and had almost disappeared by 1979. Source D tells us that public racial discrimination was banned in 1965 and that this was extended to housing and employment in 1968. This would promote racial harmony by discouraging racist comments and actions. However, Sources B and C support the view that race relations remained poor in Britain in the 1960s and 1970s [see development in previous answer]. This evidence is strengthened by the fact that the cartoon was published in one of Britain's most popular newspapers: the editors would not want to lose readers with unpopular cartoons. The photograph clearly shows ordinary working-class support for Powell rather than extremists. These men and their families may well have agreed with the racist views of Alf Garnett in the popular TV sit-com Til Death Us Do Part. Overall, the evidence strongly supports Bernie Grant's view that while race relations were legally improved, they only changed superficially among the people.

This is an excellent answer: it not only does everything the previous answer did but also considers both sides of the argument. It also considers the strength of the evidence provided by the sources when coming to an overall conclusion. It achieves this by referring to the nature, origin and purpose of the sources.

Welcome to **exam**zone

Revising for your exams can be a daunting prospect. Use this section of the book to get ideas, tips and practice to help you prepare as well as you can.

The key to success in exams and revision often lies in the right planning, so that you don't leave anything until the last minute. Use these ideas to create your personal revision plan.

Zone In!

Have you ever become so absorbed in a task that it suddenly feels entirely natural? This is a feeling familiar to many athletes and performers: it's a feeling of being 'in the zone' that helps you focus and achieve your best.

Here are our top tips for getting in the zone with your revision.

- ○ **Understand the exam process** and what revision you need to do. This will give you confidence but also help you to put things into proportion. Use the Planning Zone to create a revision plan.

- ○ **Build your confidence** by using your revision time, not just to revise the information you need to know, but also to practise the skills you need for the examination. Try answering questions in timed conditions so that you're more prepared for writing answers in the exam.

- ○ **Deal with distractions** by making a list of everything that might interfere with your revision and how you can deal with each issue. For example, revise in a room without a television, but plan breaks in your revision so that you can watch your favourite programmes.

- ○ **Share your plan with friends and family** so that they know not to distract you when you want to revise. This will mean you can have more quality time with them when you aren't revising.

- ○ **Keep healthy** by making sure you eat well and exercise, and by getting enough sleep. If your body is not in the right state, your mind won't be either – and staying up late to cram the night before the exam is likely to leave you too tired to do your best.

Planning Zone

First, fill in the dates of your examinations. Check with your teacher when these are if you're not sure. Add in any regular commitments you have. This will help you get a realistic idea of how much time you have to revise.

Know your strengths and weaknesses and assign more time to topics you find difficult – don't be tempted to leave them until the last minute.

Create a revision 'checklist' using the Know Zone lists and use them to check your knowledge and skills.

Now fill in the timetable with sensible revision slots. Chunk your revision into smaller sections to make it more manageable and less daunting. Make sure you give yourself regular breaks and plan in different activities to provide some variety.

Keep to the timetable! Put your plan up somewhere visible so you can refer back to it and check that you are on track.

In this zone, you'll find checklists to help you review what you've learned and which areas you still need to work on.

Test your knowledge

Use these checklists to test your knowledge of the main areas for each topic. If you find gaps or weaknesses in your knowledge, refer back to the relevant pages of the book.

Key Topic 1

You should know about...

❑ The British family in the 1950s **see page 9**

❑ The education system in the 1950s **see pages 10–11**

❑ Popular leisure activities in the 1950s **see pages 12–13**

❑ Living and working conditions in the 1950s **see pages 14–15**

❑ Women's work in the 1950s **see pages 16–17**

❑ Immigration and the *Windrush* generation **see pages 18–19**

❑ Racism and riots in the 1950s **see pages 20–1**

Key Topic 2

You should know about...

❑ The arguments for and against comprehensive education **see pages 25–7**

❑ The impact of changes in education on children 1960–79 **see pages 28–9**

❑ Changes in employment 1960–79 **see pages 30–1**

❑ The three-day week **see pages 32–3**

❑ The 1973 oil crisis **see pages 34–5**

❑ The 1972 and 1974 miners' strikes and the 'Winter of Discontent' **see pages 36–7**

You should know about...

- ❏ The rise of TV in the 1960s and 1970s **see page 41**
- ❏ The struggle of cinema and the press to compete with TV **see pages 42–3**
- ❏ Changes in radio and the music industry in the 1960s and 1970s **see pages 44–5**
- ❏ The rise of youth culture **see pages 46–7**
- ❏ The Beatles and the role of mass media hype **see pages 48–9**
- ❏ The Swinging Sixties **see pages 50–1**
- ❏ The impact of the swinging scene on Britain **see pages 52–3**
- ❏ Changes in leisure and entertainment in the 1960s and 1970s **see pages 54–7**

Key Topic 4

You should know about...

- ❏ The abolition of the death penalty **see pages 61–3**
- ❏ The rise of liberal attitudes **see pages 64–5**
- ❏ The extent of liberal views in Britain in the 1960s and 1970s **see pages 66–7**
- ❏ Race relations in Britain in the 1960s and 1970s **see pages 68–71**
- ❏ CND and student protests **see pages 72–3**
- ❏ Feminism and Women's Lib **see pages 74–5**
- ❏ Women in work and in politics in the 1960s and 1970s **see pages 76–7**

Working with sources

Remember, however, that this unit is not just about recalling historical information: you need to be able to interpret and make judgements about historical sources.

As you've studied each topic, you'll have built up a range of skills for working with sources. The table below lists the main areas you should now feel confident in and shows where each is covered in the book. Refer back to those pages during your revision to check and practise your source skills.

	Key Topic 1	Key Topic 2	Key Topic 3	Key Topic 4
Making inferences from sources	pages 11 and 17	pages 25 and 33	pages 47, 51, 55 and 57	pages 62, 65 and 66
Considering the purpose of a source	page 13	pages 29 and 31	pages 43 and 56	pages 67 and 75
Cross-referencing sources		page 28	pages 42 and 51	pages 70 and 77
Evaluating the reliability of sources	pages 13, 14 and 17	pages 27, 29, 35 and 37	pages 45, 51 and 55	pages 62 and 67
Evaluating a hypothesis	page 21		pages 49 and 53	pages 72 and 75

Answer All Questions

This question paper is about immigration and the problems of integration in the 1950s and 1960s.

Look carefully at the background information and Sources A–F and then answer Questions 1–5.

Question 1
Study Source A.
What can you learn from Source A about the problems faced by Caribbean immigrants in the late 1950s? (6)

Question 2
Study Source B and use your own knowledge.
What was the purpose of this representation? Use details from the cartoon and your own knowledge to explain your answer. (8)

Question 3
Study Source C and use your own knowledge.
Use Source C and your own knowledge to explain why race relations were often poor in the 1950s and 1960s. (10)

Question 4
Study Sources E and F and use your own knowledge.
How reliable are these sources as evidence of British responses to immigration in the 1950s and 1960s? Explain your answer using Sources E and F and your own knowledge. (10)

Question 5
Study Sources A, B and D and use your own knowledge.
Source D suggests that racial tension was not a major problem in the 1950s and 1960s. How far do you agree with this interpretation? Use your own knowledge, Sources A, B and D and any other sources you find helpful to explain your answer.
3 additional marks are available for spelling, punctuation and grammar. (16)

Background information

In June 1948 the SS *Empire Windrush* docked in London. This was the start of a prolonged period of immigration from the new Commonwealth. By 1961 there were 500,000, and by 1971, 1.5 million people from ethnic minorities in Britain. Many of these immigrants moved into area of big cities like London and Birmingham with cheap housing. What was the experience of these people moving to Britain and how did the British react to this change?

Source A An extract from a letter from the West Indies High Commission to the Secretary of State for the Colonies, written on 1 September 1959.

> The reports of conditions at Notting Hill continue to be the cause of great concern. We have received reports of unfair arrests of West Indians. We are concerned for those who become the victim of poor housing conditions. These decent citizens are driven into undesirable clubs, cafes and practices.

Source B A cartoon by Victor Weisz, published in the *Evening Standard* on 19 May 1959.

"THEY JUST AIN'T CIVILISED—LIKE WE ARE . . . !"

This huge addition to our population, consisting of multi-racial, largely unskilled, illiterate immigrants, was never planned or called for: it was just allowed to happen, as if it were a punishment we just had to suffer. And the social problems created by the introduction of this huge alien population into our midst are only beginning to develop.

Source D Michael de Freitas, an eyewitness at the Notting Hill riots, quoted in *History Talk Community History Newsletter* in May 2008.

The thing about the so-called Notting Hill race riots is that they were not real race riots at all. People are always fighting in an area like the ghetto; clubs are always being invaded and broken up. The general opinion was that a few Teddy Boys had simply been making a nuisance of themselves.

Source E From a speech in parliament by Conservative MP John Nott on 28 February 1968. The MPs were debating the Commonwealth Immigrants Act.

It is not about keeping Britain white. It is about keeping Britain honest. We are not divided in wanting to keep the essential characteristics of the British nation: fair play, fair mindedness and good neighbourliness. We realise that these will go if we do not control immigration.

Source F A photo taken in London in May 1968. The graffiti is in support of Enoch Powell.

wall.

Look over your revision notes and go through the checklists to remind yourself of the main areas you need to know about. Don't try to cram in too much new information at the last minute, and don't stay up late revising – you'll do better if you get a good night's sleep.

Exam Zone

What to expect in the exam paper

You will have 1 hour and 15 minutes in the examination. There will be five questions and you should answer all of these. There will be between six and eight sources in a separate source booklet; some of these will be written and some illustrations.

Question 1 is an inference question worth 6 marks. It will ask what a source is suggesting, usually phrased as 'What can you learn from Source X?' You should spend about 10 minutes on this question. For an example, see page 22.

Question 2 is a source analysis question worth 8 marks. It will ask you about the purpose of the source: 'What was the purpose of this representation?' You should spend about 12 minutes on this question. For an example, see page 23.

Question 3 is an explanation question worth 10 marks. It will ask you to use a source and your own knowledge to explain something: 'Use Source A and your own knowledge to explain why…' You should spend about 12 minutes on this question. For an example see pages 38–39.

Question 4 is worth 10 marks and asks you to evaluate the reliability of two sources. For example, 'How reliable are Sources D and E as evidence of…?' You should spend about 12 minutes on this question. For an example, see pages 58–59.

Question 5 is a judgement question worth 16 marks. It will start with an interpretation based on one of the sources and then ask 'How far do you agree with this interpretation? *Use your own knowledge, Sources A, B and C and any other sources you find helpful to explain your answer.*' Remember that there are up to 3 additional marks for spelling, punctuation and grammar for your answer to this question. You should spend about 20 minutes on this question. For an example see pages 78–79.

Meet the exam paper

This diagram shows the front cover of the exam paper. These instructions, information and advice will always appear on the front of the paper. It is worth reading it carefully now. Check you understand it and ask your teacher about anything you are not sure of.

Print your surname here and your other names afterwards. This is an additional safeguard to ensure that the exam board awards the marks to the right candidate.

Here you fill in the school's exam number.

The Unit 3 exam lasts 1 hour 15 minutes. Plan your time accordingly.

Make sure that you answer all questions.

Remember to check your spelling, punctuation and grammar when you see this.

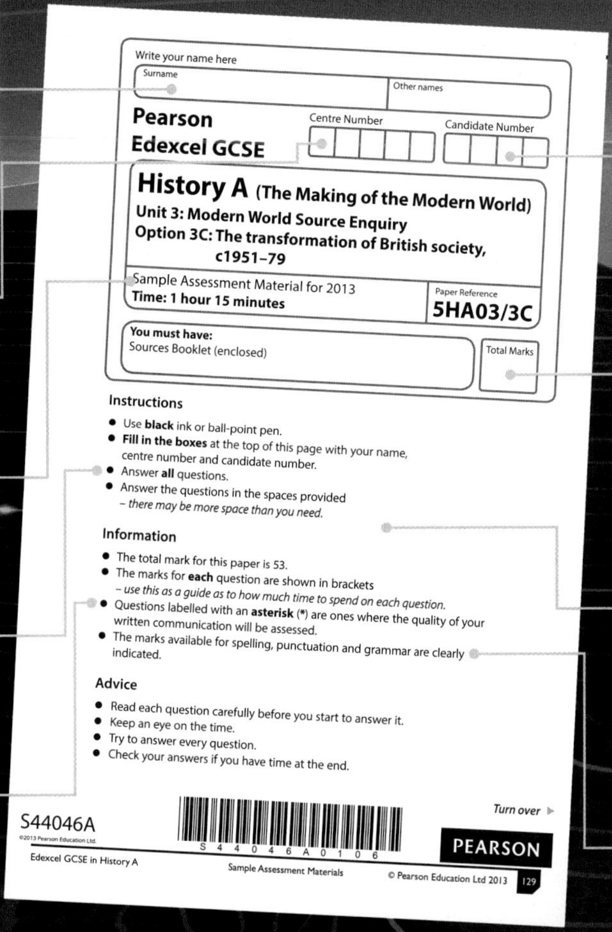

Here you fill in your personal exam number. Take care to write it accurately.

In this box, the examiner will write the total marks you have achieved in the exam paper.

Don't feel that you have to fill the answer space provided. Everybody's handwriting varies, so a long answer from you may take up as much space as a short answer from someone else.

Remember that in Question 5 the quality of your written communication will be assessed. Take time to check your spelling, punctuation and grammar and to make sure that you have expressed yourself clearly. In Unit 3 you need to answer all five questions on the paper.

Write your name here

Surname

Other names

Pearson
Edexcel GCSE

Centre Number

Candidate Number

History A (The Making of the Modern World)
Unit 3: Modern World Source Enquiry
Option 3C: The transformation of British society, c1951–79

Sample Assessment Material for 2013
Time: 1 hour 15 minutes

Paper Reference
5HA03/3C

You must have:
Sources Booklet (enclosed)

Total Marks

Instructions

- Use **black** ink or ball-point pen.
- **Fill in the boxes** at the top of this page with your name, centre number and candidate number.
- Answer **all** questions.
- Answer the questions in the spaces provided
  – there may be more space than you need.

Information

- The total mark for this paper is 53.
- The marks for **each** question are shown in brackets
  – use this as a guide as to how much time to spend on each question.
- Questions labelled with an **asterisk** (*) are ones where the quality of your written communication will be assessed.
- The marks available for spelling, punctuation and grammar are clearly indicated.

Advice

- Read each question carefully before you start to answer it.
- Keep an eye on the time.
- Try to answer every question.
- Check your answers if you have time at the end.

S44046A
©2013 Pearson Education Ltd.
Edexcel GCSE in History A

Sample Assessment Materials

Turn over ▶

PEARSON

© Pearson Education Ltd 2013   129

Answer ALL questions.

Look carefully at Sources A to F in the Sources Booklet and then answer Questions 1 to 5 which follow.

1 Study Source A.

What can you learn from Source A about working conditions for women in the 1960s?

(6)

The live question paper will contain one further page of lines.

(Total for Question 1 = 6 marks)

Each question will tell you which source or sources you need to read in the sources booklet.

The number of marks available for each question is given on the right.

Read the detail about the origin and date of each source carefully before studying the source.

Historical Enquiry: The women's movement in the 1960s and 1970s

Source A: From an interview given by Sheila Douglass for *The Sun* newspaper in 2010. She is describing working conditions for women at the Dagenham Ford car plant before the strike of 1968.

We worked as sewing machinists making seat covers for cars. It was hard work. We did the same hours as the men, clocking in at 7.30am and leaving at 5pm. We had a target of how many parts we had to stitch an hour. We worked in an old aircraft hanger. It was freezing and the roof was full of holes. We were classed as unskilled and were the worst paid. Back then it was just accepted that women got paid less than men. They thought we were cheap labour and that women wouldn't take a stand against it. But we'd had enough.

Source B: This cartoon, published in a national newspaper in the early 1970s, is a representation of the Equal Pay Act of 1970.

Zone Out

This section provides answers to the most common questions students have about what happens after they complete their exams. For more information, visit www.examzone.co.uk.

When will my results be published?

Results for GCSE examinations are issued on the third Thursday in August.

Can I get my results online?

Visit www.resultsplusdirect.co.uk, where you will find detailed student results information including the 'Edexcel Gradeometer' which demonstrates how close you were to the nearest grade boundary.

I haven't done as well as I expected. What can I do now?

First of all, talk to your teacher. After all the teaching that you have had, and the tests and internal examinations you have done, he/she is the person who best knows what grade you are capable of achieving. Take your results slip to your subject teacher, and go through the information on it in detail. If you both think that there is something wrong with the result, the school or college can apply to see your completed examination paper and then, if necessary, ask for a re-mark immediately.

Can I have a re-mark of my examination paper?

Yes, this is possible, but remember only your school or college can apply for a re-mark, not you or your parents/carers. First of all you should consider carefully whether or not to ask your school or college to make a request for a re-mark. It is worth knowing that very few re-marks result in a change to a grade, simply because a re-mark request has shown that the original marking was accurate. Check the closing date for re-marking requests with your Examinations Officer.

Bear in mind that there is no guarantee that your grades will go up if your papers are re-marked. The original mark can be confirmed or lowered, as well as raised, as a result of a re-mark.

Glossary

Term	Definition
absolute poverty	The lack of means to afford food or shelter
automation	The replacement of humans by machines in production
autonomy	Freedom to make decisions without any control or interference
boom	A period of rapid economic growth
British Commonwealth	An organisation that joins Britain and mainly former colonies of the British Empire in bonds of friendship and cooperation
British invasion	The period in the mid-1960s when British bands such as The Kinks, The Who and The Rolling Stones dominated the US 'Hot 100' chart
budget	The annual announcement by the Chancellor of the Exchequer on new economic measures
clemency	Leniency
closed shop	A system where a worker could only get a job if he also joined the trade union
decriminalised	To reduce or abolish criminal penalties for something
democratised	Having the barriers of social rank or class removed
direct grant grammar	A school where half the places were fee-paying and a quarter each paid by the government and LEA
disposable income	The money left over after all essential expenses, such as food and bills, have been paid
fascists	Relating to a political movement or party which believes that nation and race are more important than the individual. Fascist systems have an all-powerful central government and an authoritarian leader
flying pickets	Groups of strikers bussed away from their own area to form a picket line somewhere else
full employment	The maximum level of employment it is possible (or desirable) to achieve - this is always higher than 0 per cent
inflation	The rate of increase in the price of goods and services. High inflation rates would see prices rising quickly
institutional racism	Hidden policies of racial discrimination in important organisations including those run by the government
LEA	Local Education Authorities are county or borough council committees set up in 1902 to oversee education in that area.

leper	Someone with leprosy. Certain forms of this flesh-rotting disease are contagious, so historically lepers were shunned and isolated
marriage bar	A social convention that frowned upon women who continued to work once married
Mass Observation	An academic research organisation founded in 1937 that studied the everyday lives of British people
New Commonwealth	Mainly non-white areas of the British Commonwealth in Africa and Asia
OPEC	Organisation of Oil Exporting Countries. Members co-ordinate output of oil to ensure stable prices
parity of esteem	Equal feelings of pride, achievement and self-worth
permissive	An attitude that allows something to be done; in particular the toleration of sexual freedoms
picket lines	A line of striking workers that tries to prevent anyone getting into the place of work
primary immigration	A person moving to Britain alone
progressive	Favouring reform and progress rather than maintaining things the way they are
promiscuity	Having casual sexual relations with many different partners
public sector	Jobs and institutions paid for by government
referendum	A rarely used national vote on a single issue
tannoy	A loudspeaker
Teddy Boy	Teddy, short for Edward, from the Edwardian style of the boys' long coats and drainpipe trousers. Most just liked the fashion and separate identity but some formed violent and racist gangs
trade unions	Organisations which defend workers' rights and fight for better wages and working conditions
vinyl	A type of plastic used to make records. Grooves were etched into the plastic which produced music when a stylus (needle) moved over them.
vocational	Relating to and leading towards a particular career
Welfare State	A system where the government provides a range of services to promote the health and well-being of the people

Published by Pearson Education Limited, Edinburgh Gate, Harlow, Essex, CM20 2JE.

www.pearsonschoolsandfecolleges.co.uk

Copies of official specifications for all Edexcel qualifications may be found on the Edexcel website: www.edexcel.com

Text © Pearson Education Limited 2014
Typeset by HL Studios, Witney, Oxford
Cover photo/illustration © **Getty Images**: AFP

The rights of Stuart Clayton to be identified as author of this work has been asserted by him in accordance with the Copyright, Designs and Patents Act 1988.

First published 2014

17 16 15 14
10 9 8 7 6 5 4 3

British Library Cataloguing in Publication Data
A catalogue record for this book is available from the British Library.
ISBN 978 1 446906 77 4

Printed in Italy by Lego S.p.A

The publisher would like to thank the following for their kind permission to reproduce their photographs:

(Key: b-bottom; c-centre; l-left; r-right; t-top)

Alamy Images: ClassicStock 44, Pictorial Press Ltd 50, 51; **British Cartoon Archive, University of Kent** www.cartoons.ac.uk: / Solo Syndication / Associated Newspapers Ltd 21, / Daily Express 29, / John Jenson 53tl, / Solo Syndication / Associated Newspapers Ltd 57, / Express Syndication Ltd 69b; **Corbis:** Hulton Deutsch Collection 8, 19; **Courtesy, Tariq Ali Archive:** 73; **Daily Express:** Express Newspapers Syndication 42l; **Forefield Junior School, www. forefieldjuniors.co.uk:** 11; **Getty Images:** CBS Photo Archive 40, 48, Hulton Archive 42 (Inset: Derek Nimmo), 53cl, 54, 69t, 85, Hulton Archive / Bob Aylott 76, Hulton Archive / Evening Standard 35, Hulton Archive / Roger Jackson 77, Lambert 9, PIcture Post / Bert Hardy 12, Redferns / Charlie Gillett Collection 71, Science & Society Picture Library (SSPL) 65; **Image courtesy of The Advertising Archives:** 13, 17; **Mirrorpix:** 42r, 47, 72; **National Archives:** © Crown copyright, reproduced under the terms of the Open Government Licence 28; **Political Cartoon Society:** / Solo Syndication / Associated Newspapers Ltd 84; **Press Association Images:** AP / Peter Kemp 37, Michael Kappeler 18; **Rex Features:** Clive Dixon 74, Courtesy Everett Collection 45, 66, Daily Mail / Ted Blackbrow 42 (Inset: Bjorn Borg), MovieStore Collection 14, Studiocanal Films 74t, Trevor Roberts / Daily Mail 24, 32; **Science & Society Picture Library:** Manchester Daily Express 31; **See Red Womens Workshop:** 75; **TopFoto:** Action Plus / Leo Mason 55, Topham Picturepoint 60, 63

Cover images: Front: **Getty Images:** AFP

All other images © Pearson Education

Every effort has been made to trace the copyright holders and we apologise in advance for any unintentional omissions. We would be pleased to insert the appropriate acknowledgement in any subsequent edition of this publication.

We are grateful to the following for permission to reproduce copyright material:

Figures
Poster on page 65 (Source C) Family Planning Association, with permission

Tables
Table on page 16 (Source C) Women in Britain: Women, Family, Work and the State since 1945, Wiley-Blackwell (Jane Lewis) p65, 2 Jan 1992; Table on page 30 (Source B) The Office for National Statistics (ONS), licensed under the Open Government Licence v.1.0; Table on page 54 (Source B) Leisure activity table-The Symmetrical Family: Study of Work and Leisure in the London Region ,Penguin 1975 pp.212, 216 (Michael Young and Peter Willmott) 30 Oct 1975; Table on page 64 (Source B) adapted from data from the Office for National Statistics licensed under the Open Government Licence v.1.0.

Text
Extract on page 11 (Source C) The blog of poet Michael Rosen, July 2012 with permission; Extract on page 11 (Source D) Family Britain, Bloomsbury Publishing PLC (David Kynaston 2009) p.162;Extract on page 13 (Source B) Post-War Blues ref to holiday camps Living History, Leicester City Libraries (Valerie Tedder) pp.76-83, 1999, with kind permission from Valerie Tedder; Quote on page 14 (Source B) Conservative Prime Minister Harold Macmillan Party rally in July 1957, Conservative party, with kind permission from The Macmillan Trustees; Extract on page 15 (Source D) Gladys Langford- Diary of Gladys Langford,Islington Local History Centre, cited in Kynaston's Family Britain Islington Museum and Local History Centre (Gladys Langford) p.285, reproduced with kind permission of the Islington Local History Centre and Museum; Extract on page 15 (Source E) and on page 22 (Source B) from "MUNGO'S MEDALS"(1961) reproduced by permission of the National Library of Scotland; Extract on page 16 (Source A) Women and Families: An Oral History, 1940-1970 (Family, Sexuality and Social Relations in Past Times) Wiley-Blackwell (Elizabeth Roberts) p.235, 26 Feb 1995; Extract on page 16 (Source B) from Mass Observation interviews with permission from Curtis Brown; Extract on page 21 (Source D) and Introduction (Source C)The Lonely Londoners Penguin (Sam Selvon 2009) p.20-1, Courtesy of the Estate of Sam Selvon; Extract on page 25 (Source A) Circular 10/65 (1965) The Organisation of Secondary Education, Department of Education and Science London: 1965 Crown copyright material is reproduced with the permission of the Controller of HMSO and the Queen's Printer for Scotland; Extract on page 27 (Source D) Eccles & Patricroft Journal 29th August 1973, The Rev. F. R. Cooke with permission; Extract on page 27 (Source E) A Belief in How Secondary Modern Kids Could Achieve, (Catriona Nicholson), with kind permission from Catriona Nicholson; Extract on page 26 (Source C) Details from a Labour Party election pamphlet from 1964, with kind permission from the Labour Party; Extract on page 28(Source A) The Plowden Report (1967) Children and their Primary Schools Open Government Licence; Quote on page 29 (Source D) a speech in Parliament by MP for Islington George Cunningham on 5 November 1975, contains Parliamentary information licensed under the Open Parliament Licence v1.0.; Interview on page 34 (Source A) BBC interview with NUM President Joe Gormley on 13 December 1973., National Union of Mineworkers with permission; Extract on page 35 (Source B) State of Emergency p595, 598, Allen Lane (Dominic Sandbrook) September 1, 2010, Penguin Books Ltd with permission and The Wylie Agency with permission; Extract on page 36 (Source A) TV broadcast by Prime Minister Edward Heath on 7 February 1974: Conservative Party Archive at the Bodleian Library/Conservative Party Election Broadcasts from February 1974; Article on page 37 (Source C)The Guardian (Jill Tweedie), 18 January 1979., Guardian News and Media Ltd; Extract on page 43 (Source D) State of Emergency p44, Dominic Sandbrook, published by Allen Lane September 1, 2010, Penguin Books Ltd with permission; Article on page 44 (Source A) The Sun, 28 July 1967, ; Extract on page 44 (Source B) Launch of Radio 1 at 7am on 30 September 1967, The BBC with permission; Extract on page 46 (Source A) Never Had It So Good: A History of Britain from Suez to the Beatles p409-10 Little, Brown Book Group (Dominic Sandbrook) May 1, 2006, Little, Brown Book Group with permission; Extract on page 46 (Source B) from an article by George McKay], Professor George McKay with permission; Extract on page 47 (Source D) Mods and Rockers: Report from the National Association of Youth clubs, National Archives, Open Government Licence; Extract on page 49 (Source B) Never Had It So Good: A History of Britain from Suez to the Beatles Little, Brown Book Group (Dominic Sandbrook) May 1, 2006, Little, Brown Book Group with permission; Extract on page 49 (Source C) Daily Mirror published on 6 November 1963; Extract on page 49 (Source D) The Menace of Beatlism New Statesman, 28 February 1965; Article on page 51 (Source B) Top Cockneys find accents no hindrance, The Milwaukee Journal - Dec 15, 1967, Milwaukee Journal Sentinel with permission; Extract on page 52 (Source B) Sex, Drugs and Hype (Lorna Westcott) with kind permission from Lorna Westcott; Extract on page 52 (Source C) White Heat: A History of Britain in the Swinging Sixties 1964-1970 Abacus (2009) (Dominic Sandbrook), Little, Brown Book Group with permission; Extract on page 54 (Source A) New Anatomy of Britain Hodder & Stoughton Ltd p.427 (Anthony Sampson) 1 Sep 1971, Extract from New Anatomy of Britain by Anthony Sampson reprinted by permission of Peters Fraser & Dunlop (www.petersfraserdunlop.com) on behalf of the Estate of Anthony Sampson; Extract on page 56 (Source A) Y Viva España original words by Leo Rozenstraten, English words by Eddie Seago, 1974, Eddie Seago and Warner Chappell Music / Seago / Caerts / Rozenstraten with permission; Extract on page 56 (Source B) Some Liked it Hot: the British on Holiday at Home and Abroad Virgin Books 2000 (Miriam Akhtar and Steve Humphries) 9 Nov 2000, The Random House Group (UK) and Jane Turnbull's literary agency with permission; Extract on page 57(Source D) Monty Python Travel Skit- Monty Python Just the Words Methuen Publishing Ltd (Graham

A note from the publisher